LECTURES TO LIVING AUTHORS

LECTURES TO LIVING AUTHORS

By

LACON, pseud.
[E. H. LACON WATSON]

ADORNED WITH PORTRAITS
OF SOME OF THE VARIOUS SUBJECTS
BY
QUIZ

ESSAY INDEX
Essay Index Reprint Series

BOOKS FOR LIBRARIES PRESS
FREEPORT, NEW YORK

First Published 1925
Reprinted 1968

LIBRARY OF CONGRESS CATALOG CARD NUMBER:

68-54354

PRINTED IN THE UNITED STATES OF AMERICA

Contents

Contents

Sir James Matthew Barrie, Bart.

Sir James Matthew Barrie, Bart.

THE great are always surrounded by flatterers, whence it happens (as many wise men have repeatedly assured us) that they are apt to lose that salutary sense of their own insignificance which is the fount and origin of all good work. They wax fat and kick, going riotously down bypaths, when they should be employing all their energy in making a bee-line towards some lofty ideal. How seldom do they catch some far-off echo of the truth ! how rarely are their numerous defects kindly but judiciously pointed out to them ! Once in the year, perhaps, they may get a slating (as the phrase runs) in some weekly review, or even in a monthly, if they are of sufficient importance. Does this help them to a due appreciation of their sins, or discover to them in what respect they are deviating from the narrow path ? Not in the least degree ! The reviewer pinks them delicately in certain outlying portions of their anatomy, more concerned to exhibit his own skill of fence than the faults of his subject. And they themselves look through the cutting with a frown, decide that the fellow has some personal grievance or is of a bilious habit, and think as little more as they can about the matter. Few writers of my acquaintance care to linger over any press cuttings that wander beyond the narrow confines of undiluted praise.

No, the mere reviewer effects, and can effect, but little in the way of reformation. He is an inconsiderable fellow. Very often, too, especially in these weekly papers, he is jealous or has an indigestion ; he writes in haste ; he has his batch of new novels to polish off ; he is often troubled with a vague sense that he should be doing better work. With me it is a different matter altogether. I sit here, sound, healthy, and with an unbiassed judgment. I write at my leisure, of whom I will, and when I feel inclined. I am troubled neither with biliousness nor with animosity. In short, I write, in these pages, with no hope of adding to my reputation (for I shall preserve my anonymity), and with very little expectation of increasing my wealth (for I should probably spend my time more profitably in the City), but solely with the object of doing good. I stand amazed at my own nobility, but so it is.

You may reasonably ask, my dear Barrie, why I should fix upon you as the unwilling subject of my first lecture. Well, primarily because I have an admiration for your considerable talent. I chasten you because I love you, for your own good. I am the dominie, tawse in hand, and I am about to correct the whole class—though I confess I wish I could have taken some of you in hand a trifle sooner. I begin with my *dux*, as they term him in the barbaric North. Advance then, Barrie, and take it bravely. It will soon be over, and you will feel all the better for it.

And you cannot expect me to pass it over without comment when you persistently neglect your proper

work and go stealing off to those play-houses. I
expected a better example from the Head of the Class.

How purblind a creature is the general reader ! I
remember many, affecting to be critical lovers of
literature, who used glibly to discuss your merits with
me in the old days, comparing your works (and not
always to your advantage) with those of two talented
brother Scots of that epoch—S. R. Crockett and " Ian
Maclaren." Industrious romancers both, in particular Mr. Crockett, but feeding busily on a somewhat
lower slope than that on which you were wont to
graze. Wardour Street and Rampant Sentimentalism
—they have little but the Doric in common with the
creator of Thrums. Mind you, there was more than
a suspicion of the artificial-pathetic about you sometimes, but a merciful Providence preserved you from
the pit in which the late Dr. John Watson comfortably,
and profitably, wallowed. You had humanity, but
you had also a sense of humour—which was well for
you. I have seen you on occasion gambolling dan-
gerously near the edge of the gulf, but it was only in
play : you saw the danger and avoided it. How
admirable a quality is humour ! Without it you
would be even as those others, already neglected,
shabby, undistinguished.

The humorist is the only man whose pathos does
not pall. He has learned the trick of keeping his
readers oscillating upon the narrow dividing line
between tears and laughter : his is the only hand that
can guide us safely across that ledge. A man may
have wit, style, the art of phrase-making, skill in
construction of plot and in conduct of narrative, a
sense of character—and yet be but as sounding brass
or a tinkling cymbal. He may lack humour—which,

by the way, comprises much of what the Greeks meant
by the word we translate as " charity " in the Author-
ized Version.   The Complete Novelist must learn to
see men and women kindly.   He may laugh at their
weaknesses, but must love them none the less, and make
his reader love the characters he draws from them.
This, after all, is the crucial point in his art.   If he
can accomplish this simple feat, he will live after all the
intellectual gymnastics of his athletic contemporaries
have faded into oblivion.   And this is why future
generations (one or two, for I am not out to prophesy
unconditional immortality) may perhaps read your
books when the voluminous works of Mr. Crockett
and the maudlin sentiment of Dr. Watson are alike
deservedly forgotten.

But with this considerable merit, upon which I have
discoursed at such length, you have also your limitations.   Indeed, you are the most straitly limited of
all the authors of eminence with whom I am acquainted
—which is no doubt the reason why you conserved
your exiguous store of material with true Scottish
caution.   If, in our courtesy, we term you a genius,
it must be with the reservation that after all you are
but a parochial genius.   The world is not your parish
—far from it !   You cannot write far outside the limits
of your experience, and your experience has not been
particularly wide.   It might be said that you moved
with certainty in but three sharply defined plots—in
Thrums, in the half Bohemian life at the Temple or
one of the old Inns of Chancery, and in Kensington
Gardens.   Perhaps one might add also, in a house-
boat on the Thames.   In " When a Man's Single "
you give a sketch of provincial journalism as well,
which I forgot to mention.   You packed most of

your experience into that early work : it was some time before you learned the unwisdom of squandering your material with too lavish a hand.

You are pre-eminently a character-painter. With your large humanity you could not have been otherwise. Personally I am glad of it, for the true novelist of character is none too common in these days ; and in your fiction-writing days you stood as high as anyone in that category. The personages of your stories and sketches were very human, very life-like, very subtly drawn. Every good character-painter must draw largely from his own intimate knowledge of himself. The art is to conceal this, and it cannot be denied that you were never very successful in this Barrie stands confessed in almost every character you have limned with any success, from Rob Angus to T. Sandys. Barrie, of course, with a difference. I do not mean to say that you possess the fine physique of the sawyer-journalist (which would be fulsome flattery), nor that yours are the less amiable traits of Sentimental Tommy (which would be libellous), but I am very sure that you discovered all the finer touches that animate these two characters from your practice of introspective self-analysis. The adept at characterization can do this. He has a many-sided personality, from the study of which he can evolve fool or villain, hero and sage, and leave sufficient material behind for the creation of many totally distinct personages, male and female. For of a certainty he must have a feminine side to delve in as well as a masculine. When, in your Grizel, for example, you go now and again deep below the surface and return with some rare pearl of feminine speech or action, I know well that you have fished it up from your own heart.

Much may be accomplished by observation : the final illuminating touch comes only from intuition—which is introspection lit by the electric lamp of genius.

I set out to chastise you, and behold where I have arrived ! So many halfpence, so few kicks ! Well, you have faults enough, Heaven knows. Surely there never was a man with your sense of humour who possessed so little taste. Taste, I suppose I must call it, in default of a better word. Sometimes this sad failing is visible in a lack of respect for your own creations. Who but you, I wonder, after writing "The Little Minister," so admirable in its original form, would have deliberately vulgarized his handiwork by turning it into a mediocre drama ? The fact is, nothing is sacred to you. You had, possibly, an inkling of this growing trait in your character when you painted Noble Simms. It must be, I take it, the rare union of Scottish blood with the artistic temperament. And who but you would have contrived that deplorable conclusion to "Tommy and Grizel" ? In spite of a cloud of specious moralizing, that remains an artistic blunder of the first magnitude. Frankly, you got hopelessly out of your depth at the end of that story. And why ? Because you adventured into Switzerland with a lady of title. As a rule you have recognized your limitations, and that fact has been your salvation. You were not up to the task in those days. I dare say you might manage it now—but then you have given up writing novels.

In fact, it occurs to me, as I write these concluding words, that the majority of my readers will wonder vaguely what I am talking about all this time. The literary student may recollect that J. M. Barrie wrote, in the dark ages, "Auld Licht Idylls," and "A Win-

dow in Thrums," besides half a dozen other books :
the Man in the Street probably remembers nothing
of the kind : Sir James Barrie is to him naught but
a successful dramatist, the author of " Peter Pan "
and " The Admirable Crichton," of " Dear Brutus "
and " Mary Rose." But, from my point of view, the
earlier work is also the more important. If I thought
it possible that any words of mine could avail, I should
speak more forcibly than I have about the iniquity
of this philandering with the theatre. But it is too
late now, in any case. I do not suppose that we shall
ever behold you treading again the tamer paths of
letters—unless you chance to discover another Infant
Phenomenon, and write another introduction to a
Novel of the Nursery.

Mr. George Bernard Shaw

Mr. George Bernard Shaw

IT is difficult to imagine how Britain would get on without her Celtic neighbour. I confess this has always seemed to me one of the strongest arguments against separation. As things are, we have the reputation of being offensively insular and self-complacent ; what we should become without the sustained fire of ridicule and invective from the other side of St. George's Channel no man can say. Imagination shrivels at the thought. What do we not owe to the Irish ? Assuredly they are a remarkable race, who have fought by our side on many a stricken field, turning light-heartedly to worry us when for the moment we have failed to find a common foe. Misled by heraldic emblems, we English have persuaded ourselves that there is something leonine about our national character. " John Bull " was founded upon a surer inspiration. We are bovine, and an occasional rousing is good for our soul's health. This Irish terrier, persistently yapping at our heels, may sometimes goad us to frenzy, but we are good-natured at heart : we have acquired a sort of affection for the troublesome little beast : we should miss him if he teased us no longer. Without quite understanding these Irishmen, we are pathetically eager to admit that they are clever, that they possess a certain liveliness

21

of apprehension denied to ourselves. From the days of Jonathan Swift to these of Bernard Shaw, we have taken in and supported a long list of tormentors from the Sister Isle, no doubt greatly to our own advantage.

Even when we get a nasty nip in the back while engaged on some really important business we do our best to make allowances. The dog, we are eager to point out, is not really vicious : it is merely rather uncertain in temper, due to faulty handling by that keeper of ours many years ago. These Irish terriers have long memories—but we have done our level best to make up for the past.

In the meanwhile, however, you are waiting in the ante-room, which is clearly no place for a gentleman of your importance. Come right in, my dear Shaw, at once, and let us get to work. There are just one or two things I should like to say to you before you descend again to the level of the street. I have friends who would prefer to reason with you in a different manner. Among the Philistines you were never exactly popular, and your behaviour during the war did not raise you in their estimation. They failed to realize that you could not be happy unless you were outraging the most sacred feelings of a hated majority. I used to spend much valuable time in those days apologizing on your behalf and explaining away your conduct. To paraphrase old Samuel Johnson, I would not have you put in the pillory : the fellow has too much literature for that. The Muses shall come to the rescue of their child.

" There are few living writers whose works are so stimulating to the imagination as those of Bernard Shaw." I take these words from the publishers' advertisement on the cover of " The Doctor's Dilemma," under which name one of your volumes of plays was brought out in 1911. For once in a way the publisher's appreciation may be endorsed by the critic. It is juſt. Whatever your faults, you are undoubtedly ſtimulating. We may not agree with your conclusions : it is extremely probable that we shall quarrel with your taſte ; but, if we possess brains at all, you will make us think. This is your mission in life, and you have been at it now for a good many years : ever since, in faćt, you came up to London in 1876, at the modeſt age of twenty, to combine Socialiſt agitation with criticism of the fine arts. For I can remember the time when you wrote " The Quintessence of Ibsenism" and "The Perfećt Wagnerite," and delighted readers of the *Star* and the *World* with musical criticism, as also that rather later period when you illuminated the columns of the *Saturday Review* with comments on the drama of the day. Also you joined the Fabian Society, the year after its foundation, and contributed not a little to the fame of that combative asssociation by editing the " Fabian Essays." In all these capacities you displayed, at leaſt, the faculty of arousing attention : you had something to say, if not always ſtrićtly germane to the subjećt supposed to be under discussion. And your manner of saying it was indisputably arreſting.

The journaliſt, as was almoſt inevitable, developed into a noveliſt, but your attempts in the direćtion of fićtion did not find an immediate or remunerative market. However, " The Irrational Knot " and " Love among the Artiſts " appeared as serials in a certain magazine condućted by Mrs. Annie Besant. Another periodical, no longer exiſting, printed " Cashel Byron's Profession " and " An Unsocial Socialiſt."

These things happened in the early eighties : it was not until 1892 that your firſt play, " Widowers' Houses," was produced at the Royalty under the auspices of the so-called Independent Theatre.   Some ten years later came the famous Vedrenne-Barker management at the Court, and the markét in Shaw shares began to boom.   The new playwright became a Cult.   The ſtuff was not only popular on the ſtage, but the published copies sold more readily than moſt novels.   Not to admit the aſtounding cleverness of the plays was to be " out of the movement," and no doubt, in accordance with the beſt traditions of the country, many excellent but ſtupid persons in the higheſt circles attended the performances religiously, and pretended to enjoy what they entirely failed to underſtand.

I recolleƈt on one occasion hearing you explain why you had turned from the bookſtall to the ſtage. As might be expeƈted, you were very frank and shameless about the matter.   There was no money in novels, and there was a great deal of money in the theatre, and while Providence arranged things like that a sane man had but one course open to him— he muſt follow the cash.   Where you used to get hundreds from the publisher you now got thousands from the theatrical agent, and you cheerfully advised all of us (for we were an audience of authors) to go and do likewise.   I think some of us followed your advice at the earlieſt opportunity : at any rate, it is noticeable that since that diſtant address of yours a conſtantly increasing phalanx of prominent noveliſts have marched on to the boards, reaping, no doubt, a due financial reward.

What precisely is your position to-day in the

theatrical world ? I wonder whether you will ever recapture that early success, born partly of curiosity, partly of fashion, that made your box-office receipts so pleasant a subject of contemplation to you in those old pre-war days. You will have an occasional revival, of course, but I fancy the Shaw boom will not revisit these islands. Nevertheless, there should be no cause for dissatisfaction. Your plays will live as literature—for a time.

They are, I think, better in the library than on the stage. In fact, you are one of the very few dramatists who can be read with pleasure. The majority are unreadable by anybody—unless by those enthusiasts who will read anything remotely connected with the theatre. The ordinary dramatist requires the services of real men and women to vitalize his conceptions. His plays are made by the actors, whereas yours would still be interesting if performed by the veriest amateurs. Recognizing this, you take care to cater for the reader in your stage directions, which are not only remarkably explicit, but contain an abundance of little humorous touches that linger pleasantly in the memory. Take that of the trousers of a certain character in " Man and Superman," which were " neither black nor perceptibly blue, of one of those indefinitely mixed hues which the modern clothier has produced to harmonize with the religions of respectable men." Or again this description of the old servant at the opening of " The Doctor's Dilemma," who " has used her ugliness to secure indulgences unattainable by Cleopatra or Fair Rosamund, and has the further great advantage over them that age increases her qualification instead of impairing it." These literary felicities of description enable us to see the characters of your plays with a sympathetic underſtanding. On the ſtage they are loſt, and we are by so much the poorer. I think your dramas should be read firſt and seen afterwards.

You achieved your success, like many of your compatriots, by treading on every one's toes. You were, in short, a bully—an intellectual bully—holding the moſt unpopular opinions you could find, and professing not the smalleſt respect for any of the cuſtomary conventions—modeſty among them. You were convinced that Bernard Shaw was a great man ; you knew yourself to have a following of ardent and fashionable disciples : why, then, pretend that you were unacquainted with these obvious facts ? Thus we used to hear you speaking quite openly and candidly about Shaw's philosophy and the Shavians—a word that you invented yourself to denote those who followed in your train. This peculiarity alone would be enough to frighten moſt sober Englishmen ; but then you take occasion, in the excellent but lengthy prefaces prefixed to all your published plays, to run a tilt againſt every eſtablished belief they have ever possessed. Take the volume containing " John Bull's Other Island," and " Major Barbara," in which you give a dissertation, some fifteen chapters long, on such subjects as separation and the British occupation of Egypt, moſt diſtressing to all sound Imperialiſts ; and another, nearly as long, on such controversial topics as the Salvation Army, and Chriſtianity and Anarchism, at leaſt equally diſtressing to all sound Churchmen. Then, too, you muſt have your way in every little thing : you muſt needs issue special inſtructions to your printers to eliminate all signs of the possessive, or of contractions, all inverted commas and italics, so that the very look of one of your works oppresses the reader with a sense of strangeness and unfamiliarity. Consider also that you are a Vegetarian, an Anti-Vivisectionist, a Socialist—all sorts of unpopular things—and that you have seldom missed an opportunity to gibe at Imperialism and Vaccination, and it must be conceded that you did very well to attain the point of general acceptance that was yours ten or eleven years ago.

Whether your reputation stands as high now as it did in 1914 is another question. Probably not. In times of peace it does not matter so much that you should invariably contrive to associate yourself with the unpopular side. No previous national crises would have been considered quite complete without you prodding the quivering hide of the people with your venomous pen. You were one of those nuisances that had become established by long usage, like the Derby dog : any suggestion that you should have been led off to the lethal chamber would have excited indignant letters to the paper and a Shaw Defence League. But this war was a serious matter : we did not want a jester, licensed or otherwise, writing letters to point out that there was not really very much to choose between the enemy and ourselves. It says a great deal for the privileged position you had acquired that you escaped assassination.

The bulk of your writing is a personal explanation. You are not particularly in love with the dramatic form. It would be well enough if you could go on the boards yourself, and play the hero all the time ; but even with you there are certain limitations. I imagine you prefer oratory to any other method of disseminating your opinions, though I have heard you deny that you are a good speaker. Oratory permits digression (provided the speaker has an interesting personality), and you like diverging into scraps of autobiography and reminiscence at a moment's notice. By now you must have learned that to take up the unexpected view on every subject you handle is a difficult pose to maintain, but you keep it up nobly : by perpetual hunting after paradox you now and again stumble upon something that has the air of a strange truth. Born in 1856, you should soon be shedding some of your playful combativeness. But you will have to live a long time before you become as other men.

Perhaps, after a lapse of some years, I may modify these last words. There are signs in your more recent work of a growing humanity. I think you are less of the mischievous imp now : you have more sympathy with your fellows. After all, yours is the type of mind that commonly mellows with age—and even a vegetarian feels the approach of seventy. I think it will be agreed, when critics of the future attempt an estimate of your actual position in the world of letters, that " Saint Joan " has in it more of real value than most of your earlier works.

Mr. Herbert George Wells

Mr. Herbert George Wells

YOU have been, it seems to me, a singularly fortunate man in your early environment, for a writer. It is a great thing, in this overcrowded profession of ours, to be able to strike out an entirely new line, to tap a fresh source of inspiration, to interpret to the great world of readers a stratum of our complex society that has hitherto been overlooked. The Man who Knows must always be in demand.

I discovered once, when I was looking into the details of your career for my own base ends—it is surprising to reflect upon the number of times that I have been asked to write something on your work —that besides being more or less a contemporary of my own you were also (this was where I began to envy your opportunities) the son of Joseph Wells, professional cricketer. Strange to reflect that you, who wrote scoffingly once of " Mr. Flack," that " bat in the Corinthian style, rich and voluminous," should have sprung from such a source ! Possibly you drew thence that contempt for mere games that peeps out here and there in your works : you may have seen, and heard, too much of them in early youth. Thus it comes that you shall so hardly persuade the son of a clergyman to attend Divine Service.

All the same, I should have liked that parental trade.   It should have given you an insight into many things.   Indeed, it undoubtedly did : much of those early days no doubt went into " The New Machiavelli " and many other works.   Wells *père*, perhaps fortunately for posterity, was neither the Hobbs nor the Parkin of his day : he played occasionally for the county team, but did not make a fortune from the game.   (The day of the " expert " journalist was not yet.)   Consequently, his brilliant son had the chance of gaining an insight into certain walks of life (including that of a draper's assistant) which has proved eminently useful to him in his chosen profession.   All novelists work more or less upon the foundation of their personal experiences : with some the process is more obvious than with others, but no man relies wholly upon his imagination.   Indeed, useful as is this quality, it cannot function without some support : like a creeping plant it requires a trellis of wooden fact to raise it above the earth and enable it to put forth decorative blooms.

Education, as we perceived in many books even before " Joan and Peter," is a subject that interests you enormously, as indeed it cannot but interest any intelligent man.   I take it your own experience of schools was not altogether fortunate, and probably left you with a healthy animus against the whole tribe of schoolmasters that was only partially dissipated when you came across the remarkable personality of the late Mr. Sanderson, of Oundle.   You began, apparently, by taking on the job of pupil teacher at a school in Somerset : went, after an interval spent in drapery on the South Coast, to Midhurst Grammar School as an assistant master, and finally, after winning a scholarship at South Kensington and taking a B.Sc. honours degree, as a Science Master at a school in St. John's Wood. The various places of education so lovingly described in your novels perhaps owe something of their life-like naturalness to these wanderings.

From teaching to the writing of books is a simple transition. Indeed, you are essentially a propagandist : you have never stopped trying to instruct the world, and I sincerely hope that you may yet go on teaching and preaching for many years to come. You began, naturally enough, by producing a biological textbook, which is, I believe, the only book of yours that remains, and is likely to remain, unread by me. But your first definite literary success came from the publication of a metaphysical article in the *Fortnightly Review*. That was in 1890 : from that you went on to write for the *Globe*, the *Saturday Review*, the *National Observer* and the *Pall Mall Gazette*. I can remember when you were dramatic critic for the *Pall Mall*—a circumstance that provided material for one of your earliest short stories, " The Obliterated Man."

This was the period of the short story. Fashions come and go, in literature as in other fields of activity. At the end of the last century, for a space of about ten years, this form was in the mode, attracting the most brilliant of those young writers who have since become middle-aged, or dead. In the nineties Kipling and Barrie had just appeared upon the scene : every one was talking of " Plain Tales from the Hills " or "A Window in Thrums " ; and most of us were trying to do something of the same sort ourselves. I have heard that it was Mr. Lewis Hind, then editing the weekly *Pall Mall Budget*, who first suggested to you that this form was worth trying. There followed a time of rapid development. Short ſtories, by your own account, came to you readily enough : they appeared out of the infinite, in surprising fashion : for several years the flow continued, with scarcely an effort on your own part ; and then the ſtream ceased, as suddenly as it had begun. It was almoſt as though some one had turned off the tap. I suspeċt myself that you felt, with that reſtless and inquiring mind of yours, that you were getting into a groove, and it is very much to your credit that you have always abhorred grooves. I am not sure that it is not your chief title to fame.

The beginning of the present century found you experimenting with the fantaſtic. We had seen " The Time Machine," " The Wonderful Visit," " The Island of Dr. Moreau," " The Invisible Man," and had welcomed at any rate a commercial success with " The War of the Worlds" and " When the Sleeper Wakes." Also you had diſturbed the reviewers, who prefer a certain homogeneity in an author's work, by intercalating two novels having more relation to real life—" The Wheels of Chance" and " Love and Mr. Lewisham." Juſt about then you ſtood on the brink of " arriving," as the phrase used to run in those days. Anxious critics were waiting, ſtop-watch in hand, to time your entrance within the sacred portals. It seemed that you were in no hurry. You chose that occasion to take a very ill-assorted pair of travellers on a journey to the moon, and followed up this vagary with the firſt of your sociological works, bearing the somewhat cumbrous title of " Anticipations of the Reaċtion of Mechanical and Scientific Progress upon Human Life and Thought." We may imagine the anxious critics pocketing their watches again with a sigh. Here was a man not subject to the common rule, who would have to be judged by standards other than the ordinary. Was he going to fritter away his undeniable talents from a lack of concentration ? He might have been another and a greater Jules Verne, for he had a gift of characterization denied to the Gallic idol of our youth—and here he was writing a serious work on social problems. Did the man, by any chance, imagine himself a Thinker ?

Since those far-off days we have had many novels from your pen, and with ordinary luck we may hope to have many more. But I suspect you have finished with the fantastic : you have sown your wild oats in those strange regions outside our limits of Time and Space. Let us admit that you did those stories as well as need be—perhaps as well as they could be done. It is your chief praise that you never permitted the wealth of your inventive imagination, even in its wildest flights, to obscure the humanity of your men and women. We are always more interested in the persons than in the machinery. Recalling the days of our boyhood, we shall find that with the ingenious Frenchman it was precisely the opposite. He also sent a party of travellers on a voyage to the moon : it is interesting to compare the two volumes. M. Jules Verne paid far more attention to the Columbiad and its padded projectile than to the three gentlemen who allowed themselves to be shut up within its walls ; but with Mr. Wells we let the scientific part yield in interest to Cavor and his companion. They are much more alive than President Barbicane, Michel Ardan, or Nicholls. But then their creator is alive too— quite extraordinarily alive.

I suppose " Kipps " was the book in which you really " found yourself " for the first time. How long ago " Kipps " seems now, and how many volumes have we not seen between that admirable work and your latest gigantesque endeavour. I believe I have read all of them. I should not like to miss a Wells : there is sure to be something in it worth remembering —something stimulating and provocative. You take hold of the latest problem of modern life and handle it after your own fashion, like a terrier with a bone. You fully intend to crack it somehow and get at the marrow inside. Reviewers may object to your methods, but for the future at any rate one novelist is not going to submit to any restrictions. Modern fiction must take all life for her province, sparing neither sex nor creeds.

But the great thing about you, in my opinion, is that you have continued to grow. For a novelist, success commonly means an arrested development : the world, his agent and his publisher all conspire to persuade him that he has gone far enough, and that for the future he had better make an honest living by imitating himself. From an artistic point of view his career usually ceases at the moment when his commercial success begins. You are not liable to this reproach. Possibly it may be held that you err slightly in the other extreme : just when we are thinking that at last you have evolved the one form that suits you to perfection you are off experimenting with a new medium, with fresh combinations. A gallant spirit, and assuredly the right spirit in which to do good work, but sometimes a trifle disconcerting ot the critic. For it is not merely that you are apt to change your methods, but your views are no longer what they were when the slow-witted reviewer read the success of laſt season. No sooner has the patient classi-fier got his tray ready and his labels, and approached the victim ſtealthily, with the idea of assigning him his juſt place in the scheme of the universe, than some subtle change, hitherto unseen, forces itself upon his notice. Moſt remarkable ! when we saw him before we thought he was rather one of the shining lights of that society : now, for all our dull wits can see, he is laughing at them. Clearly we muſt reserve our judgment, and put our labels away for the present. But it is all rather unsettling.

This is one reason why you are the moſt ſtimulating writer we possess at the present moment. You refuse to be bound by anything you may have said on a previous occasion. Consiſtency, that dull and much overrated quality, is not for you. The great need is for Growth : we muſt develop, not ſtand ſtill nor revolve in circles. Thus you take up with each new movement as it comes along, extract from it the essential juice (for in the moſt futile of them all there is always to be found at leaſt a flavouring for the eclectic palate), and pass on gaily to the next. One happy result of this conſtant movement is—that you are always very much in earneſt. You are not deterred from saying juſt what you think by any considerations of expediency. You do not care if you offend your readers nor are you anxious to harmonize your words with anything you may have written before. Nor, I may add, have you any great tenderness for the feelings of paſt workers in the same field. You may have been intimate with them in the paſt, but if you consider, on calm reflection, that they are now making themselves slightly ridiculous, you have no

hesitation in saying so.   Personally, I should not care
to be too intimate a friend of yours : a spice of apprehension would mingle with the pleasure I felt on
opening the latest Wells.   There are those who say
that you have treated some of your past friends rather
scurvily—in print.

That, no doubt, is the result of possessing such
power of observation.   From your works the future
historian should be able, with due limitations, to
reconstruct with curious accuracy the middle-class
England of the late nineteenth and early twentieth
centuries.   I say, " with due limitations," for there
are certain sections of society in this country with
which your sympathies have always been imperfect,
which you seem to observe with a half-conscious squint,
perhaps with a superficial accuracy but with no real
and understanding vision.   You have never been
able to take an impartial view of the Public School,
the Universities, the Country Gentleman.   If a man
has the misfortune to have passed through what used
to be called a " liberal education," he starts, in your
eyes, with a grievous handicap.   Perhaps I should
say that he used to start, for you have modified some
of these views of late.   I believe you are not so certain
as of old that a Cambridge Etonian is necessarily an
offensive ass, or that a clergyman must clearly be a
fool or a hypocrite, or both.   You even showed signs,
some years ago, of sympathy with the worries of an
episcopate.

There is a good deal of the schoolmaster about you
even now.   They say it is extraordinarily difficult to
get rid of the stigmata of this profession.   Your conversation is apt to be didactic.   A friend of mine
once complained that you did not argue : you delivered

opinions.   It is not easy to arouse your curiosity :
you are more interested in your own thoughts than
in your companion's.   You do not speak as well as you
write.   But then it must be admitted that you write
very well indeed.

NO. IV

Mr. John Galsworthy

Mr. John Galsworthy

THERE is not much to be gathered of your career from the useful pages of " Who's Who." A reticent character yours, not in the least anxious to give away to a curious crowd of readers particulars of parentage or education or place of birth. We are not even told whether you prefer lawn tennis to golf, though we should be a little surprised to learn that you cared much for either. Just a list of works is all I can find in my copy of the handbook. True, it is not the latest edition, and it is possible you may have grown more communicative since the close of the Great War, but I do not think it likely.

Born in 1867, I suppose you were examining public school life at Harrow about the time that I was doing the same at Winchester. But, unlike so many Harrovians who have taken to the writing of fiction, you do not seem to have written a story of your own schooldays. I suspect you of too much reserve for that. Most novel-writers give themselves away in their books, but the writer of school stories is apt to do so more than any—for he has to begin so young if his work is to have any value. His is a difficult task, to steer a safe course between the Scylla of sentiment and the Charybdis of cynicism—too difficult for anyone below the ripe age of thirty.

43

Then, I suppose, you " ate your dinners," even as
I did myself, and were called to the bar, which I was
not.   I like to think of you sitting there in hall, a
young man of twenty years or so, tight-lipped and
silent, observing everything and not saying much to
anybody.   There was plenty of time, and a great
deal to learn about human nature.   You had no intention of rushing headlong into print, like some hyster-
ical schoolgirl.

Not until you were thirty-one did you publish a
novel.   And even then, so cautious were you that you
adopted a pen-name.   I remember, about the time
of the South African War, hearing of a young man
called " John Sinjohn " whose work was worthy of
some attention.   After two or three years he faded
away, and I wondered what had become of him.   But
he had not been cut off in his prime.   The promise
of his youth was not to remain unfulfilled.   The
author of " Jocelyn " and " A Man of Devon " was
to rise again, under his rightful name, as the author of
" The Man of Property."   Which, as every intelligent reader knows to-day, is the opening book of that
remarkable series dealing with the family of Forsyte,
the greater part of which is now bound together in a
single volume and procurable at the ordinary price
charged for an ordinary novel.

It is by this Forsyte Saga that you will live—or at
any rate deserve to live in our remembrance as one of
the true succession.   A wonderful work !   A vast
panorama of the last half century, into which you
poured all that you had seen and noted during those
early years, all that you had guessed or divined.   The
mid-Victorian age is there, preserved like some mam-
moth that stepped incautiously upon a soft bank of

yielding prehistoric clay, and slowly sank therein, to
its immediate discomfort but ultimate preservation.
Our London is there, from the days of peg-top trousers
and crinolines and the Prince Consort, down through
hansom cabs and bicycles and the Boer War, to motors
and aeroplanes and a Labour Government. And the
story is not yet finished, for which we are duly grate-
ful. Indeed, if we possessed a really far-seeing
Government, who can doubt that it would insist on
paying you several thousands a year as a retaining
fee on condition that you continued the history of
the Forsyte family (which is also the history of the
Upper-Middle Class of this great Empire) so long as
you were able to write at all ?

Failing that, " The White Monkey " will do to go
on with.

We are an ungrateful generation. I heard the
other evening, from the lips of a lady of some intelligence next to whom I happened to be sitting at dinner,
that " The White Monkey " was an artistic error.
That picture of Soames Forsyte sitting alone in the
oasis he discovered up in Highgate Cemetery and
passing in review the history of the family should have
been left undisturbed : to call him out again into the
pages of a book was something like insisting on an
actor coming before the curtain and bowing his
acknowledgments when he had breathed his last on
the stage. That is what she said—and also some
hard things about " Beyond " and " Saint's Progress."
But she was not a real Galsworthian, and I did not
argue the point. I have learned the deep unwisdom
of arguing about books. A book, like a new acquaintance, either takes your fancy or not. If you force a
favourite author down the throat of a friend you are

doing neither of them a kindness. For my own part, when anyone says to me, " You *must* read Dash : he is far and away the best man writing novels to-day," I feel at once an instinctive dislike for the fellow.

And I suppose an appreciation of your works is not universal, even among those who pride themselves on knowing good stuff when they see it. To my mind —let me confess at once and be done with it—this Forsyte Saga of yours is a bigger thing than has been done by any of our contemporary novelists. There is astonishingly little I could wish altered in it. And, as so often happens, my admiration for this work has thrown a glamour over the rest : I read virtues into them that perhaps are not really there : faults that irritate others seem to me trifling, matters of no moment. Yet at the same time I can see easily enough an attitude of mind that might annoy some. You would not have appealed to the old-fashioned Englishman of our grandfathers' time, who liked his bit of hunting and shooting without worrying his simple soul too much about how it felt to the fox or the pheasant. As well get into a stew every time he sent a poacher to gaol at petty sessions.

This humanity of ours is a modern plant. Not even yet does its cultivation make for popularity. Like stout old Lord Romfrey in " Beauchamp's Career," many of us nourish a distrust of humanitarian principles, beneath which we suspect something of the crank. No unnecessary cruelty, if you like, but if we once begin questioning the justice of imprisonment for fraud or things of that kind, where are we ? The foundations of society would rock beneath every Forsyte of us all.

I confess I should never have predicted for you
that commercial success that you seem to have attained.
I should have put you down as too quiet, too unemo-
tional, to capture the general public.   But sometimes,
by a fortunate chance, this public of ours does forsake
its usual habits : overtaken by a sort of madness, it
runs wild after the strangest gods, for a time.   And
in one of these paroxysms it appears to have picked
up this pale, grey, clean-shaven barrister, who under-
states all his points rather than the opposite (and the
public was always supposed to prefer a touch of
exaggeration), and at the least hint of unfairness or
bullying invariably ranges himself on the weaker side.
I dare say the plays helped.   A play or two, produced
at a London theatre and discussed over tea-tables,
does indubitably help to advertise a man.   And then
you were so intellectual in appearance.   Just then, I
suppose, the public thought it would like a little intel-
lect for a change.

You have a desire for justice so tyrannous that it is
reflected in every part of your personality.   You look
like a man who passes many sleepless nights weighing
carefully the two sides that are fated to complicate
every question.   There is so much to be said on both
of them—especially on behalf of the unpopular.   I
take it this is why the critic notes a certain drab quality
in your works.   They are painted, to use the terminology of a sister art, in a low key : there are no
thorough-paced villains to be found, and no glorious,
immaculate heroes.   Well ! for my part I like grey
tones.   Life is like that.   In the good old days it was
required of all writers that they should be blind of one
eye.   Journalists and novelists alike had to have their
convictions, and stick to them.   To hint that there

might be some excuse for any action on the part of the opposite side in politics was a mistake that your editor would be extremely unlikely to overlook : to try and arouse your readers' sympathy for the bad man of your novel was regarded by your publisher as an act almost equally reprehensible.   We were children then, and believed in bright colours and the cardinal virtues.   Art critics were only just beginning to talk of Values.

Some call you grey, and imagine it a term of reproach.   True enough that you have a tenderness for the pathetic stop.   But you handle it so extraordinarily well that all but the fiercest critics acknowledge your right to pull it out when you like.   *Mentem mortalia tangunt* should be your motto.   And just beneath the unshed tears lies always a note of comedy, seizable by the cool and detached observer.   I fancy this restraint of yours, that refuses to let pathos have its way unchecked, that is always ready to record the intermingling humour, gives your work much of its peculiar and individual charm.   I have jotted down at different times a hundred examples.   Let me quote a tiny instance—culled from the " Indian Summer "—where old Jolyon and Irene are together at Robin's Hill :

"There, there—there, there ! " he murmured ; and putting out his hand reverently, touched her.   She turned, and leaned the arms that covered her face against him.   Old Jolyon stood very still, keeping one thin hand on her shoulder.   Let her cry her heart out—it would do her good !   And the dog Balthasar, puzzled, sat down on his stern to examine them."

That is all !   Observe, if you will, that it is just one single word, slightly unusual in this connection, that gives the necessary jolt to the mind already becom-

ing attuned to the sentimental mood. (The word
"stern," I mean.) It is sufficient. There are those
who accuse you of unnecessary fullness, of all a law-
yer's anxiety to include every single detail that can
have any bearing on the story, but to my mind you
have a rare sense of economy in words. I have seldom
known you use too many—in your big scenes.

(When you are deliberately trying to be funny it is
different. There is one passage some eighty pages
earlier that I should like to delete entirely. I cannot
imagine how you ever let it pass. But there it is !
And, as it is the only one I dislike, I shall say no more
about it here.)

I have said nothing of your plays. They would be
better, I think, if your sense of humour were a little
keener. But your outlook on life has always been
intensely serious. Usually you have some thesis to
expound in your plays, some evil to expose or some
reform to advocate, and in the plays it is more difficult
to disguise this than in a novel. It resolves itself
generally into a game of " loading the dice " against
the particular piece of social injustice you wish to fight.
In your anxiety to secure justice you tend to become
unfair against the dog who is uppermost for the
moment. When I read " Justice " or " Strife " or
" The Silver Box " I cannot help feeling that everything is being " managed " to throw the existing state
of society into the worst possible light.

I do not think you a great dramatist. Frankly, I
am rather surprised that your plays have done as well
as they have. You take the unpopular side every
time, and the public used not to care about paying to
hear sermons. Sometimes, as in " The Forest," you
seem to have run off the lines of common sense alto-

D

gether.   Nor do I regard you by any means as a great
writer of short stories.   But you are a great novelist
—perhaps the greatest we have to-day.   And that
should be fame enough for a single man.

NO. V

Sir Arthur Conan Doyle

Sir Arthur Conan Doyle

WE approach with you, my dear Sir Arthur, a distinctively British subject—probably because, with that wrong-headedness characteristic of your race, you chose to be of Irish extraction, born and educated in Scotland. That nothing might be omitted from your make-up, you were sent to Stonyhurst, of all places in this wide world, before settling down at Edinburgh to read for your medical degree. Yet, in spite of these inexplicable happenings, I never look upon you but I perceive a successful Englishman, rather of the old school. I picture you as a Northern farmer, breeding fat stock in the vales of Westmoreland, and succeeding better than your neighbours because of that touch of imagination that differentiates you from your fellows. (I suppose it is just that distinguishing touch that comes from your Irish ancestry.)

I take it you would have succeeded in any branch of industry you might have chosen to adorn. For all branches of industry, singular as it may seem, are the better for this same quality of imagination, so long as it is strictly controlled. And you have always had the invaluable faculty of keeping yours in thorough restraint. It is never permitted to go rioting over untried turnips, starting no end of game that we cannot pursue at the moment, like a badly trained setter. Mr. Gilbert Chesterton is not so careful with his—but I propose to call him up for judgment later.

A stranger, meeting you for the first time, would not be likely to suspect you of authorship. He would perceive a massive, bulky personality with the air of a prosperous country squire. You might be a company director, head of a big engineering firm, or merely a hard-working county magistrate ; but assuredly you do not look the sort of person to have created the ingenious and imperturbable Holmes, the gallant Brigadier Gerard. Your conversation does not, at first, appear to coruscate with any superficial sparkle. Solidity, I should say, was your outstanding characteristic. You have the gift of concentration, and it has enabled you to do many things more than commonly well.

When you take anything up, you do so in no half-hearted spirit. Whether you are playing billiards, or golf, or taking the chair at a public dinner, or delivering an address on Spiritualism, you give your undivided attention to the business in hand. You may have little particular natural aptitude for any of these things, but you were always a firm believer in the value of constant practice. By virtue of steady trying you made yourself into a distinctly creditable cricketer, good enough to take part occasionally in first-class matches. You have entered for the Amateur Championship at billiards—and were not knocked out in the first round. Were it not for the intrusion of so many new interests lately, you might well bring your handicap down to scratch at golf.

I mention all these things, not from any desire to annoy you (for I know nobody in the world of letters whom I regard with a more affectionate respect), nor even from a foolish wish to indulge in idle gossip, but because I conceive they have a distinct bearing upon the position you have attained in this difficult profession of ours. You have reached your present exalted rank by sheer hard work. Mind you, I do not hint for a moment that you were destitute of ability at the start. But you have made the very best of your talents. You had hard work to get a hearing—which is often a blessing in disguise for us who write—and you learned early that an infinite capacity for taking pains, though it may not mean genius, often produces similar results. Some account of your early struggles may be useful to the adventurer in literature. In your "Memories and Adventures" you have thoughtfully furnished him with all the detail he can want.

The Doyle family has supplied us with several artists, though before your own time they were famous rather with brush and pencil than with the pen. Your grandfather was John Doyle ("H. B."), who has been called the father of polite caricature, and the signature of your youngest uncle may still be observed by the careful student on the cover of *Punch*. Your father, too, was a painter of more than ordinary merit, but apparently he did not possess your driving force. Perhaps the air of Scotland was just what was required to give the right mixture for a writer of stories of adventure.

It must be a great point to possess the Celtic love of a fight tempered with a dash of Scottish caution and solidity. That forthright narrative of yours I put down to the Edinburgh influence : we feel sometimes that without the counterbalancing Irish element it might have become a trifle heavy.   This side saw, too, that you never missed knowingly an opportunity for adventure.   You took on your first serious job, as surgeon of the whaler *Hope*, at less than a week's notice : after seven months in the Arctic you tried another surgeon's berth, in the *Mayumba*, trading to the West Coast of Africa.   All this had its value as Experience, without which the best of us are as naught.   But even while you were working as a student your first contribution to literature made its appearance, in *Chambers' Journal*, which must by now have acquired something of a reputation for printing the early works of the undiscovered great.

This contribution was a short story called " The Mystery of the Sassassa Valley," and it was a considerable time before it was followed up by another attempt. After your experiences on the *Hope* and the *Mayumba*, and a short interlude in partnership (which also bore fruit afterwards) you settled down to make a living as a general practitioner in Southsea, writing short stories in your " all too numerous leisure hours."   But anonymity was then the order of the day in our chief magazines, and after seven years' hard labour your name was no better known to the general public than it had been at the start.   Probably it was this that decided you to let Messrs. Ward Lock buy outright the copyright of " A Study in Scarlet " for twenty-five pounds—which is all you ever got for the book in which the great Holmes made his bow to the public. He was, by the way, Sherringford instead of Sherlock in the first draft.

But it was " Micah Clarke " that first brought you real fame, and as this was published in the same year as " A Study in Scarlet," it may reasonably be regarded as a twin first book. I believe you spoke of it as such when, many years ago, Mr. Jerome K. Jerome's magazine, *The Idler*, invited you to contribute the story of your literary career to a series. Yet this admirable story of Sedgemoor and the Monmouth rebellion, finished in 1888, was a long time before it found a refuge at Longman's at the instance of Andrew Lang. " Blackwood found that the people did not talk so in the seventeenth century : Bentley that its principal defect was that there was a complete absence of interest : Cassell that experience had shown that an historical novel could never be a commercial success." Young novelists may well take heart when they read these words. For when the historic house of Longmans did at last accept the book, it was at once acclaimed as the best historical novel written for many years. It has, I believe, been since adapted for school use—a compliment not often paid to modern fiction. I confess I have never seen the school edition, and cannot therefore say in what particulars, if any, it differs from the common form. But where it is in use, pupils must look forward with a flattering eagerness to the reign of the second James.

In the early nineties " The Adventures of Sherlock Holmes " started on their long course in the *Strand* magazine. With intervals, the great detective has been appearing almost ever since in those familiar pages. The astonishing success of these stories has perhaps done something to obscure your real merit as a novelist. They made your name as widely known as that of any contemporary writer, but the usual penalty followed a sudden reputation. Editors, publishers and the public wanted more Holmes, and still more—to the exclusion of anything else. It was no good planning an elaborate death : the man might die, but this (as careful editors pointed out) was almost a necessary preliminary to the publication of his memoirs. Dr. Watson, unhappily, still lived, and his piety was such that he might be expected to continue glorifying his dead friend for all time.

Some of the Sherlock Holmes stories were very good of their kind : others, it must be confessed, were not so good : one or two showed a lack of intimate acquaintance with the life they professed to describe, surprising in so generally careful a worker. For in " The White Company " and " Micah Clarke " you had obviously taken immense pains to acquaint yourself with the periods. You may have made an occasional error in terminology, but it was not from want of reading up the subject. I have heard that you spent a year in reading before you began to write " Micah Clarke," and you saturated yourself with the literature of the epoch before adventuring on " The White Company." Yet it could never be said of you that your information was unduly obtruded. Your writing was always simple, natural, and to the point. It is noticeable that in " The White Company " and " Sir Nigel " there is little trace of that Wardour Street English in dialogue or narrative which most writers would have considered essential to a proper treatment of the fourteenth century. And you had the crowning merit of opening your stories well. Before three pages are read we come upon some striking picture that stands out and gives the keynote of the book, like the expulsion of John of Hordle from the monastery, or the old soldier of fortune coming to the house of Cornet Clarke.

I have sometimes wondered whether, as time went

on, you did not begin to shirk the hard labour of
preparation. Probably you found that you could no
longer spare the time. Your succeeding novels
showed a tendency to degenerate into mere sketches
of interesting periods. They lacked the spacious
atmosphere of the earlier books : they were altogether
conceived on a smaller scale ; and, although they
were still good reading, they displayed a rather melancholy reluctance to grapple boldly with a big subject
and carry it through to a satisfactory conclusion.
" Rodney Stone," for example, is in many ways an
excellent study of the prize ring and of the palmy
days of the Regency. But the story is at once weak
and melodramatic—almost as melodramatic as that
of " Uncle Bernac," which is perhaps the least satisfactory of all the books of this epoch. These two, in
fact, together with " The Tragedy of the Korosko "
and " The Hound of the Baskervilles," are little more
than short stories expanded into suitable size for a
volume. They are the immediate result of popularity
and big sales. Yet there is something good in the
worst of them. Even in your verse (which is certainly
not your strongest suit) there is to be found here and
there a happy thought couched in vigorous and manly
language.

Your medical experiences were turned to account
in a volume of stories called " Round the Red Lamp "
and in a more important book, " The Stark Munro
Letters," published by Longmans in 1895. The
form of this story has possibly militated against its
popularity, for we do not much love fiction by corre-
spondence. But these doctor's reminiscences are
very well worth reading, not only for the realistic
account of the young man's early fight for recognition,

but for the very life-like sketch of Cullingworth, the
genius with the methods of a charlatan. The book,
too, contains a larger proportion than most of your
particular humour—a brand of humour that is far
from being subtle or in any way difficult of apprehension, but is always provocative of healthy laughter.
The merit of your humour lies in a quick sense of the
incongruous, and a simple, straightforward manner
of exposing it. It is good-natured, sound common
sense, that delights in shearing through a sophism or
in unmasking pretentiousness. The companionship
of the young Canadian and the officer of the Court at
Versailles in " The Refugees " is fruitful in plain,
sensible repartee of this kind. You have always
employed the good old English brand of humour,
which condescends at times to farcical incident, as
when Master Tetheridge is found hiding in the
meal-chest after Sedgemoor ; or to the repetition of
some stock phrase, such as Sir Nigel Loring's " pros-
pect of honourable advancement," or his friend Sir
Oliver's perpetual reference to fat pullets.

You are the novelist of the average Briton, and of
the male rather than the female. You do not elaborate
your psychological analysis : you deal chiefly with the
obvious : your opinions are for the most part what we
call sound—that is, they harmonize with those of the
majority. Observe, I separate from these remarks
on your novels anything I might have to say on the
subject of Spiritualism. But into that elusive subject
also you have imported all your ancient qualities. I
am not quite sure that the reading world would not
prefer to see your victorious common sense employed
in another series of Sherlock Holmes or the gallant
Gerard. But this form of research has appealed to

you : something of the proselytizing fever of the convert has seized a brain that always flamed at the thought of injustice.   I am not with those who scoff at you on this account.   Whatever you do, I am very sure it will be intended to further the general good of humanity.

I have left myself no space to deal with your merits as a war historian.   They are very considerable— from the popular point of view.   You have the art of narrative : you can reduce the tangled happenings of a campaign to a more or less connected story suitable for family reading.   Nor can I discuss your plays, your verse, your excursions into literary criticism.   You have made your experiments, but the historical novel remains the field on which you have scored your real successes.   I have heard you say, characteristically enough, that " The Cloister and the Hearth " was the finest novel in the English language.

Mr. Walter De La Mare

Mr. Walter De La Mare

YOU were born in 1873, say the books, and had to struggle to make a name, as indeed have most of us who pursue the glorious trade of writing in any form, but especially those who dally with serious verse. (One of the pieces of advice that I should give to every literary beginner is that he should accustom himself to the writing of verse—but by no means to take it seriously. If he does, he is clearly bound to become either a poet or a failure, and failures are much commoner than poets in this imperfect world.) I suppose you took the making of your verse with a sufficient seriousness, but there has generally been a touch of the humorous about it as well, or of the fantastic. It is as though you were playing at being a lonely child, meditative in a garden. You had never really been taught to play with the others, and they seemed to avoid you. You were queer to them—an oddity ; but it did not seem to bother you much : you continued to play on by yourself, crooning strange songs. It came to pass, after some time, that a few of them imitated you, but not many, and seldom with any success. A certain type of mind was requisite for the reproduction of that dreamy wistfulness which has always been your chief charm.

Some people cannot understand it. I have known excellent fellows, good general judges of literature, who have examined your poems with puzzled faces, wondering "what he was trying to get at," and, still more, what other critics could find to praise in it. Yet, somehow or other, your poetry seems to have won its way to a certain popularity. I do not imagine you will grow wealthy on it, but you have excellent reviews from the critics, and the bulk of your verse has been published in two fair volumes.

It is only of late years that we have heard much of your name. I am told you spent the better part of your youth in the City. They talk glibly of a commercial employ and its sad effect upon those skylarks who would fain soar upwards into the empyrean, but I am inclined to think some steady job of the clerkly kind is an excellent thing for your budding poet. It supplies the rocks and boulders, without which the progress of the stream would be so painfully uneventful. It also prevents him from rushing into print too hastily, by giving him plenty of other things to do. This is why your first book did not come out till 1902, when you were nearly thirty years of age, and why only a few had heard of you until just before the Great War.

You were doing journalistic work, at first. I can remember one "Walter Ramal," an anagrammatic pseudonym which covered several of your contributions to the press in those days. I imagine you did a lot of reviewing, in papers like the *Bookman* and the Literary Supplement of *The Times*. Reviewing may sometimes prove a soul-clogging task, but it has its value, and perhaps especially for the young poet. It makes him pay a certain attention to form and the necessity of that discipline which he is preaching to others. You must have done a prodigious amount of critical work, and you did it all as it ought to be done—not grudgingly and of necessity but as though you really liked doing it and took a pride in carrying out the weekly task with fine critical judgment in your own distinguished style.

I do not think I ever came across you personally in those journalistic days. We were both free lances, I suppose—that is to say we were not definitely bound to the fortunes of any single editorial office—and probably you were never a great frequenter of literary clubs. But I have some recollection of seeing your name, I think, in the *English Review*, and one or two other magazines. Then I saw some reviews of "Henry Brocken," and tried to read the book, and thought it rather difficult stuff.

The fact is, you are one of those originals who will insist upon pursuing a way of their own with everything they undertake. To the ordinary man, like myself, such beings are Cranks ; and it takes us a long while to appreciate their real value. It is only after many years and much travail of soul that we learn how important the Crank is to the scheme of the universe. Without him we should probably never progress at all. He is the motive power behind every revolution. But then there is also the Freak, and he is indubitably a person of less importance to the world, and on occasion a source of legitimate amusement. It is not always easy for the young man to distinguish between the Crank and the Freak, and I confess I classed you for some time in the second category. What did you want with writing a thing that looked like a novel and was nothing of the kind,

peopled with a lot of characters out of other books ?
All very poetic and fanciful, no doubt, but we do not
care for poetic fantasy unless we are warned it is
coming. Sprung upon us in the guise of something
else it merely offends. So far as I remember, I never
finished " Henry Brocken " at all.

But I do think " The Midget " is a fine book, in
its way. No one else could have done it but you.
I own frankly that, had it not been for " The Midget,"
I should never have included you in this motley
collection. I have my doubts about the wisdom of
it now. The habit of my mind is entirely alien from
yours. I am apt to pride myself on a catholic taste
in letters, but I have read the whole of your two
volumes of collected verse without being moved to
anything more enthusiastic than a feeling of tepid
appreciation here and there. And when I see the
critics writing a lot of stuff about elves and fairies,
fauns and dryads and whimsical dreamings I begin,
with the best will in the world, to mistrust the author.
Why is he dealing with things like these at his time
of life ? And this, you will agree, is not the right
sort of spirit in which to compose a sober and responsible lecture, that should be useful to the subject
himself, as well as to the general reader.

Mr. Enoch Arnold Bennett

Mr. Enoch Arnold Bennett

FEW, I imagine, are aware of your first name, which indeed is not aggressively obtruded upon public notice. There are some who cherish an objection to biblical names, and it cannot be contested that a spice of roguery attaches to some of them—for example Jabez, Ebenezer, and Zerubbabel. Enoch, however, is by comparison harmless, and would have made a striking and uncommon substitute for Arnold, had you elected to make use of it. He, too, was translated—no bad omen for the budding author. Still, the name of a writer, as of most public men, is so much a matter of association that we need quarrel with no man's choice : a great novelist can dignify that of Dickens ; a bad one will not be greatly helped by the sounding patronymic of Fortescue or Seymour. Arnold Bennett is by way of shedding lustre on the family name. You are, I suppose, Bennett the Great ; and though your signature contains thirteen letters (which the superstitious reckon a serious handicap in the race for success) you contrived to win fame and fortune at a reasonably early age.

The books state that you were born in 1867, in the district which you have celebrated with so creditable an industry. The Potteries, as this part of North

Staffordshire is called, consists of half a dozen towns lying so close together that they seem to form a single city ; and under the Potteries Federation Scheme of 1910 they were actually amalgamated to form the municipal borough of Stoke-upon-Trent. Burslem and Hanley are the other two important members of the " Five Towns," and it is with these that the novels are chiefly concerned. You selected a dingy centre of industry, but one not without historic associations to the student of British ceramics. Josiah Wedgwood was born at Burslem in 1730 : Josiah Spode the second (Biblical names appear to have been popular in the Potteries) at Stoke-upon-Trent in 1754, where also the great house of Minton arose and flourished.

And once, no doubt, it was beautiful. Staffordshire has many natural advantages, but the hand of man has lain heavy on the soil : coal, and iron, and pottery works have blackened the face of the countryside, turning the greater part of it into a dingy wilderness of grimy buildings. Few live there but those who are compelled to do so by the claims of business ; and the consequence is that there has grown up in these towns a race of beings somewhat different from the ordinary, retaining certain of the old habits and modes of thought practised by our Victorian ancestors.

Indisputably it is an advantage for the novelist to have a district that he can make his own. The British Isles are parcelled out by now pretty thoroughly among the growing band of fiction writers, but since the days of George Eliot we have had few to paint the humours of the midland counties. That excellent and ingenious lady was Warwickshire bred : she confined herself for the most part to that county, with a slice of Leicester and the southern part of Stafford-

shire. I cannot recall many others who can be said
to have exploited the midlands with any thoroughness,
in the same way as Thomas Hardy has exploited
Wessex, or Eden Philpotts his little section of Dart-
moor. So your choice of country had the merit of
freshness. And you were a native : the five towns
were familiar to you from your youth : you could
not fail of a real sympathy with their inhabitants.
It has been yours to introduce and interpret to the
world that singular congeries of provincials. You
have, of course, touched on other subjects as well,
but not often. Like most sensible writers, you prefer
dealing with the familiar.

Your path to literary fame led through the thorny
ways of journalism. I think it must have been about
1893 that you became connected with a certain ladies'
paper, which you afterwards edited with some success ;
and it was five years later that there came to me for
review one of your earliest works, in which you endea-
voured to instruct your fair clients how best to pursue
the path you had yourself travelled so recently. " Journalism for Women " was the name of the volume, and
the author's name was given as E. A. Bennett. I
confess that at first I reviewed the book under the
impression that the editor of *Woman* was a lady.
So well, even at that early date, had the coming
novelist learned the trick of identifying himself with
the characters he described.

I take you to be one of those rare men of letters
who are capable of writing, at will, to please the
popular taste. It was said of you that, at an early
stage in your career, you resolved to do certain books
for your support—" pot-boilers," as they are playfully
but often inaccurately termed in art circles—and cer-

tain other books to please yourself and to enhance
your reputation among the critics.   I do not say that
this resolution of yours was uncommon :   many
writers, no doubt, have determined at various times
to follow a like sensible course ;   but it is diſtin&tly
unusual for anyone to carry such an intention to a
successful conclusion.   Moſt of us, I suspe&t, are so
miſtruſtful of the public taſte in letters that we imagine
popularity can be secured by careless and slipshod
work ;   and when we aim at this simple method of
pleasing the great body of readers we find, to our
disguſt, that we have merely succeeded in alienating
the reviewer, hitherto our only friend.   The fa&t is,
no writer can work happily at anything but his normal
level :   he cannot " write down " to his public ;   and
any attempt at this sort of condescension will do him
more harm than good.   He can, however, vary his
theme and his methods, within certain limits ;   and
it seems to me that you have managed to do this very
cleverly.   Your lighter ſtories, such as " The Great
Babylon Hotel," " Buried Alive," " The Card " or
" The Regent," are as carefully conſtru&ted as your
more serious ſtories of the order of " Clayhanger "
or " Hilda Lessways," but they commonly deal with
a farcical subje&t and are handled in a bright and
irresponsible ſtyle.   In their own kind, they are admirably done :   it is not in the leaſt surprising that they
should have achieved their primary purpose of money-
making.   What perhaps is a little surprising is the
fa&t that you should have succeeded also in the second
part of your scheme, securing a reputation with your
serious work that brought you to the front at once
as one of the moſt considerable noveliſts of the day.
    You came to your own with curious suddenness—

or so it seemed to us who were watching with interest
your career in fiction.   But general recognition suffers
as a rule so many inexplicable delays that we are apt
to regard it as sudden when at length it actually arrives.
Most of us, your brother craftsmen, had made up our
minds that the name of Bennett was not as well known
to the general public as it deserved to be.   You had,
it seemed, a fair sale, but the outside world had not
yet begun to talk of you.   Known favourably in
literary circles, you had not yet become the theme of
general conversation in the drawing-rooms of Belgravia
or Mayfair.

Some of your books, even then—" The Old Wives'
Tale " for example—were said by some critics to
possess elements of greatness.   But it was reserved
for " Clayhanger " (published, I believe, about the
end of 1910) to mark the epoch of your arrival, your
ceremonious entrance into the palace of the successful
artist.   As though by general consent every one began
to talk of Arnold Bennett, and the name has been
on the lips of the world of readers ever since.   Yet
" Clayhanger " hardly seems now the sort of book
that we might expect to take the world by storm.
It is a good piece of work enough, but rather a slice
cut from life than a constructed story : it is long, full
of detail, destitute of startling adventure, inconclusive.
The characters are drawn from a stratum of society
with which few novel-readers are acquainted—with
which few, one would have said, desired to make acquaintance.   The story was true to life, and that is indubitably a great merit, but many books have possessed
it and yet failed to find a remunerative sale.

And, in fact, at any other time in your career it is
probable that the publication of " Clayhanger " would

have brought you little more than a sheaf of more or less favourable notices. The particular work on which a novelist (or other artist) emerges into public notice is not always intrinsically superior to those that have preceded it : the moment of its appearance is often of more importance than anything else. For the writer of real worth begins by building underground for many years, laying his foundation on the solid rock. Sometimes, indeed, he has been known to go too deep, with the result that he never appears above the surface at all ; his work may be of the best, but it never becomes visible to the general public ; only his friends are aware that he is labouring there, placing carefully one well-shaped stone upon another. Give him life enough, and the quality of perseverance, and in due time he suddenly becomes visible, though the last stone on which he takes his stand may be no finer or larger than many of those that had gone before. It may also be sadly admitted that this surprising emergence into the light of day after years of total obscurity is apt to prove rather too much for some of us, whose subsequent work has not been improved by our popularity.

I do not, however, accuse you of having been spoiled in any way by success. You seem to me to have pursued your wonted path since that event, much in the same way as before. During the war you were decidedly not so vocal as Mr. Wells, between whom and yourself there has always been a spice of healthy rivalry. But then it would have been difficult indeed for any less agile writer to have kept pace with the creator of Mr. Britling and Joan and Peter, who found time also to dally with the souls of bishops and to write a modern version of the Book of Job.

You wrote little, save in the way of journalistic propaganda. But then it must be borne in mind that you have succumbed to the glamour of the footlights, which Wells has hitherto successfully evaded.

I conceive you to have displayed something of a genius for commerce. There are points about you (as is not unnatural) that remind me of your famous Alderman, Mr. Edward Henry Machin. You, too, saw possibilities in the stage. You discovered, too, a most admirable and ingenious method of using the same story more than once—a method so simple that one wonders no one had the intelligence to discover it before. You wrote "Clayhanger," and then "Hilda Lessways," which is the same novel from the point of view of the woman instead of the man. There seems to be no limit to the developments that may arise out of this interesting departure : it points to a new form of the novel altogether, and it may be admitted that some new form of fiction is greatly needed. We waste a great many admirable characters in our books, placing them in subordinate positions where they have no opportunity of making a real and intimate impression upon our readers : now it may be possible to take them up again, making them the protagonists instead of mere accessories, and without being at the pains to contrive a new plot for their benefit. Indeed, we have seen recently that it is not even necessary to confine ourselves to our own disused characters : we may, with Sir Harry Johnston, try our hand on someone else's. But to do that, I take it, requires the nerve of a retired pro-consul.

This happy invention of yours should have made you a popular man among those of your own profession. Not that you were ever in danger of unpopularity, but you are too seldom seen now with your brethren of the writing craft.   The theatre, I suppose, has prior claims.   And you always had something of a shy and retiring disposition.   Several of your characters are masterpieces as studies of that nervous temperament which is capable, through sheer anxiety to escape notice, of performing the most remarkable actions.   Nor were you ever the readiest of speakers. Like other celebrated writers, Charles Lamb and Charles Kingsley among them, you have a slight hesitation of speech combined with a lisp which is rather engaging.   It is, I think sometimes, a mistake for an author to be too fluent a talker ; and you shall often find that those who by some accident or other have acquired a tendency to play the part of listener reap a certain advantage over their more garrulous brethren.   They reflect more : they have more time for observation : perhaps they save a good deal of useful material that the others allow to run to waste. This may be, in part, the secret of your success as an observer of life.

For you are probably the most acute observer writing novels to-day.   Your stories are almost too full of detail—as full as a Dutch interior by some old master—but it is undeniable that you get effects that way.   " Riceyman Steps " and the short story of " Elsie and the Child " describe furniture with the minuteness and accuracy of a flash-light photograph. Perhaps the method is growing on you.   I do not quarrel with it : I am catholic enough in taste to admire a character like Elsie, by whatever means obtained. But I have a fancy that some of my brother critics are disposed to regard you as too material for their finer souls.

You have done all sorts of writing, like a good journalist. (I am not sure about poetry, but I suspect, like most of us, you dabbled even in that when young.) They tell me you have also the agreeable talent of painting in water-colour. Truly the good fairies must have been in the ascendant when you were born. Withal, you used to be a pleasant companion, in the far-off days when we sometimes met. I am sorry that I so rarely come across you now.

NO VIII

Mr. Gilbert Keith Chesterton

Mr. Gilbert Keith Chesterton

IT must have been some ten years before the war that I had the honour of meeting you for the first time, in the smoking room of a certain London club. Not many members were there that evening, and it so chanced that (in a kindly spirit) I made some casual remark. The big stranger was looking just a trifle bored : in fact, for the moment you were without a listener. My almost accidental pressure of the button sufficed to set things going : for the next hour and a half you talked without ceasing : doubtless you would have exceeded this modest span if I had not been compelled to get home early that night. My recollection of you has always been dominated by that chance meeting. I seem to see you now, with your back to the fireplace, your forehead corrugated with a thoughtful frown above your glasses, declaiming to me your opinions on things in general. Even then you were a man of weight, though not so bulky as you have since become, if we are to trust the photographers. Your style of speech was best described by the single word " copious." You advanced upon any fortuitous listener with the unanswerable massive weight of an elephant, but of an elephant richly decorated, with howdah and trappings gaily gilt. I take it you must have been quite young at that time.

We regarded you in those days as something of an infant phenomenon. As a matter of fact, I suppose you must have been thirty or thereabouts, even then. You were born, say the reference books, on the twenty-ninth of May, in the year eighteen hundred and seventy-four, and you left St. Paul's School, Hammersmith (where you had already acquired something of a reputation as an exponent of the Socratic method of reasoning), seventeen years later. There was a short time when you had some idea of becoming an artist in another field, and for awhile the Slade school sheltered you. But that remarkable flow of words was not to be denied. Journalism was so clearly your trade that there could never have been any serious doubt as to your future career. Almost at once the stately portals of the press were flung wide open to receive you. The *Bookman* welcomed you as an art critic : the great Liberal papers, the *Speaker* and the *Daily News*, opened their arms to a recruit at once so youthful and so dogmatic. The art of design assumed, with proud humility, a back seat. But you have published drawings, or caricatures. Complaisant reviewers declared them to be not without merit.

There was no doubt of it : we all thought in those far-off days, the beginning of the twentieth century, that we had found a new literary star of unusual brilliance. You arrived with dramatic suddenness. Scarcely had we begun to ask who was the owner of those mystic initials, G. K. C., that cropped up so often in the *Daily News* of that period, than we found the full name confronting us in a hundred places, writing about all sorts of things, enunciating and defending paradoxes on every conceivable subject. Literary and artistic criticism, discussions on ethics and

religion, a weekly causerie for an illustrated paper—
and then, perhaps, a volume of fugitive verse and
another of amorphous fiction. The name of Chesterton became an obsession, a literary nightmare ; there
was no getting away from this new, voluminous,
comprehensive personality. You wrote the first of
your novels, if indeed they can be called novels,
" The Napoleon of Notting Hill " : you did Browning
for the English Men of Letters series : you gave the
world your ideas about Charles Dickens. When
you were barely four-and-thirty years old these works
had already excited sufficient interest to induce the
publication of a volume estimating your position in the
hierarchy of letters. In 1908 appeared " G. K.
Chesterton : a Criticism."

There was a time when to think of the name Chesterton was to recall also that of Hilaire Belloc. A sort
of amiable rivalry used to exist between the pair in
their efforts to put the world straight. But Belloc
is the older of the two : he has sat in Parliament, and
lost many of his earlier illusions : during the war he
degenerated into a Military Expert. His was the
more subtle method, when the two of you were pleasantly engaged in attempting to reform the universe.
He was wont to tickle the British public under the
ribs with the two-edged knife of irony, while you
belaboured their thick hide with the resounding club
of paradox. I suppose you may have stirred a few
from their slumbers. They may not have felt the
blows, but they heard them ; and some began to ask
each other, in a sort of amazement, what on earth the
fat man with glasses and a double chin was making
such a fuss about.

For a success in letters it is indeed useful to acquire

the reputation of a madman, even of a charlatan.   It can hardly fail to arouse controversy : your admirers will rally round you : your enemies will advance gaily to the attack, and the rising dust of the conflict will prove the best of advertisements.   There is nothing like dividing the world on the great question of your own abilities.   And with regard to yourself there were never any half measures : a man was either a Chestertonian or not : either he took everything you wrote and asked eagerly for more, or he expressed to his friends astonishment at the impudence of a fellow who should try to palm off such ridiculous rubbish under the name of literature.   I have had men coming to me almost with tears in their eyes, entreating me to explain what there was about you to make some of the papers so enthusiastic.   Could anybody really take you seriously ?   They would admit perhaps that here and there, in the mad web of your work, patches might be discoverable of fine prose, not merely well expressed but containing a modicum of stimulating thought.   But what a form !   These unexpected and disturbing ornaments came in the middle of a sort of story, something that had the outward guise of a novel, but of a novel written in a lunatic asylum.   A sort of harlequinade of the strangest characters, doing the most unexpected and impossible things, most trying to the equanimity of the ordinary reader who had hoped to lose himself in the windings of a pleasant tale.

I used to explain that yours was a curious character. You were a Preacher, who for some obscure reason cast your sermons into the outward form of novels. It did not really much matter—except that it deceived some of the unthinking populace.   Except for the outer husk, these books of yours were not in the least

like fiction by any of the recognized masters. The
ordinary reader, chancing upon " Manalive," let me
say, or some other of your more recent works, would
be much in the position of a lover of plain chocolate
who found himself biting unexpectedly into a slab of
similar appearance filled with some strange liqueur.
There is a sort of story in the book ; there are even
characters, masquerading in the clothes of men and
women. But they bear no relation to real life. Their
duty is merely to provide the talented author with a
few pegs on which he may hang the particular sermon
he is so anxious to deliver. I do not know why you
should have chosen this form, but so it is, and we must
make the best of it. I confess that I find it difficult
to read these grotesque fantasies with any patience,
but I am quite ready to recognize that there are good
things scattered here and there in their pages. They
have the air, somehow, of having been composed in a
spirit of bravado, as though the writer were laughing
in his sleeve and saying, " Look at me. I can do
anything I like, and persuade the world and the critics
that it is great."

You were the spoiled child of English literature.
You may survive it, becoming, like other infant pheno-
mena, a respectable member of society now that the
dangerous period is over. In fact, I dare say that you
have already survived it, but I have not read anything
of yours very recently, and so cannot say whether you
still disport yourself in print like an expert funambulist
on the tight rope. In the old days, you know, the
majority of us thought you a *poseur*. It was almost
inevitable. Your admirers turned the limelight upon
your massive form with so much industry that, in
mere self-defence, you had to be prepared for the

blinding glare at any moment. Was ever a young
man so quoted, so caricatured, so peftered with invita-
tions to deliver himself at societies and clubs on the
Subjeft of the Moment, whether it were female suffrage
or pure beer ?   You represented the great Dr. Johnson at a pageant : it was said that the likeness was
unmistakable : you were marked down as his lineal
successor, the diftator of literary London.   Well, well
—if you have really got over all this without serious
damage it is perhaps due to the war intervening.   If
it has not yet provided a world fit for heroes to live
in it has at leaft amended our sense of proportion.

Alas ! my Chefterton, you and I are alike no longer
young, in years.   You preserve, however, a specious
appearance of youthful energy.   It is possible you
may ftill shed a few skins.   It is possible you may
decide to exploit a new form.   For you have plenty
to say, but no vehicle at present that will carry it easily.
I wonder you do not try the ftage.   Why not become
our English Ariftophanes ?   For you have something
more than a mere talent for verse : I would sooner
read a volume of your songs than one of your deteftive
ftories.   You are a natural singer, but you never have
been able to tell a ftory.

I suppose it may be held a measure of the enthusiasm
you inspire in your followers that some were found
to maintain that those deteftive ftories of yours,
collefted under the title " The Innocence of Father
Brown," were the finest deteftive ftories ever written.
Frankly, they were nothing of the kind : they were
very bad deteftive ftories indeed : there was not a
thrill in the round dozen of them.   But they were
packed with ingenuity.   About many of them were
quite admirable patches of descriptive writing.   To

say that the most nervous of maiden aunts could take the volume to bed with her and read them before she fell asleep, would perhaps be nothing were it not that you were obviously trying to make our flesh creep. There is scarcely one of these stories that does not contain one or more violent or sudden deaths. In the hands of Poe, or Stevenson, or Conan Doyle, these could hardly have failed to send a shiver through us ; with you they left us unmoved, self-possessed, a trifle critical. All the materials were there, together with an account of literary skill all too rare in those who affect this form of fiction, and yet the tales missed fire.

Of course, they were ridiculously improbable. In itself this is not of the greatest importance. Most detective stories are ridiculously improbable, when you come to analyse them with the cold eye of criticism. But the writer must contrive somehow to make them plausible at the time : he must throw a glamour over them : at the worst he must contrive to dull the critical faculty by importing a measure of horror into the mystery. The cold, logical manner of Edgar Poe is better for this purpose than the gay, debonair method of G. K. Chesterton. It throws a detective story out of focus. But more important than either the richness of your manner or the improbability of your plot was your failure to make any of the characters alive.

This is, it seems to me, the crucial defect in all your books that I have read. You are more interested in yourself and your own thoughts than in humanity. For all that, you are a stimulating writer. Full of vitality, an opulent nature, a big man, with big ideas. After all, luxuriance of imagination is not too common a fault. At present you seem to some of us like an elephant gambolling in a suburban back garden, a spectacle somewhat disturbing to those critics who believe in law, order and restraint.   But some day you may discover your proper form, and work miracles.

Mr. Robert Smythe Hichens

Mr. Robert Smythe Hichens

THERE was once a singular institution called, somewhat grandiloquently, the London School of Journalism. I gather from the public press that schools purporting to teach the art of writing, journalistic or other, flourish even in the present day : there may even, by now, be another bearing the same title. They arise, and fade, and rise again. And there is, I suppose, a certain part of the journalistic trade that can actually be taught—given a teacher who knows his business. At the worst the anxious beginner can be cautioned against certain offences—against the unblushing use of outworn clichés, or of the split infinitive. But why you should have frequented the school in question I cannot say. Possibly you thought, in those early days, that there really was a Mystery of Journalism to which the initiated might provide a key. Possibly it was already clear to you that the school itself might be productive, in the future, of good copy. Or it may be that parental foresight insisted upon this ante-chamber to Bohemia, to make sure that your character should not be ruined by a too early and facile success. In any case you became a pupil, together with at least one other writer of reputation, Mr. Francis Gribble. Genius, we know, will out : it is as difficult to conceal as murder : as hard to eradicate as hereditary gout. Probably the easy methods of the ingenious gentleman who ran the establishment did little either to improve or impair the style of these eminent authors.

The curious may find this same School of Journalism portrayed, with little more than a touch of caricature, in the pages of " Felix," a novel in which there is more autobiography than we are accustomed to find in your works. Perhaps for this reason, I have always regarded it as one of your best books. It came at a fortunate period, when you had already written enough to gain command of your material, and before you had acquired the verbosity that distinguished some of your later novels.

You are one of the few literary men who know something about music. Many authors have dabbled in painting : not many have been attracted by the mysteries of harmony and counterpoint. Samuel Butler, it is true, advanced some way up both avenues ; but at the moment I can recall no other name to brigade with yours. For it was your earliest ambition to become a musical composer, and you actually went through a course of study for that purpose at Bristol and in London. If, at the ripe age of thirty, you had not made a hit with " The Green Carnation," it is possible that you might have achieved fame by another route. But " The Green Carnation " set people talking. It was a clever book, of a kind that often attains success through curiosity. Several well-known persons, Oscar Wilde among the number, were understood to be discoverable in its pages, under a thin disguise. The *roman à clef* has often proved the propriety of its name by unlocking the gates of Fame's fore-court.

Perhaps it dates you a little to say that the book was published in 1894. We were both young then, and the literary world had its fashions no less than it has now. Men, and women, now dead or forgotten, were in the forefront of the new movement : magazines and reviews sprang up like mushrooms in the night : little poets produced slim books of verse, even as they do now ; and brilliant young writers coruscated in somewhat artificial prose under the fostering wing of the late W. E. Henley, then editor of the *National Observer.* There followed, during the next three years, " An Imaginative Man," " The Folly of Eustace," " Flames," and " The Londoners." I have often wondered, especially now that you have attained to a certain success in the theatrical world, why this last book has never been adapted for the stage. The earlier part of it is admirable farce, carried on with immense spirit. Towards the end, it is true, it degenerates into a sort of knockabout humour. But it possesses a charming young American lady masquerading in man's clothes who should make the fortune of any play.

With added years came a sort of seriousness. Did you despise the precious gift of humour ; or did it merely fade away, as such gifts will ? The faculty for writing farce seemed to have been lost when, in 1901, you published that melancholy attempt at boisterous fun, " The Prophet of Berkeley Square." It seems almost incredible that this book could have been written by the same hand that produced " The Londoners." Some of the critics began to express doubts as to your future. Would you prove yet one more of that band of young writers who were destined not to redeem their early promise ? However, you pulled yourself together and gave them " Felix," which was much better stuff. I do not say that it is a great novel, but it will bear reading more than once—which is more than can be said of most novels in these degenerate days. It has characterization : there is pathos to be found in it as well as humour. The critics revised their opinion, and agreed that you might still go far.

In a sense, I suppose, you have, though it must be confessed that your more recent books have not shown an improvement commensurate with your increased years. You have " arrived," it is true. Just twenty years ago you brought out " The Garden of Allah," and your name was made. Incidentally you discovered a formula—always a dangerous discovery for an artist to make. Put in a few words, that formula may be stated as The Importance of the Elderly Woman. Before your happy arrival she had been neglected by the novelist : her fading charms were treated with levity or, even worse, with an exaggerated sympathy. And yet the lady of forty to fifty years felt within herself that she still had the capacity for adventure : she saw no reason why she should retire so early into the background and be content to watch her younger rivals taking all the prominent parts. Women were beginning to emancipate themselves : year by year they were growing determinedly younger, especially if they chanced to be unmarried. Yet it was undeniable that the dreaded borderland of Middle Age was near at hand : they snatched, with a courage born of despair, at the chance of one real adventure before quitting the arena. It was Hichens who had the wit to perceive this cardinal fact, and to turn it to his own advantage. While your comrades blindly

concentrated their energies on the young and un-
formed heroine you struck out boldly into the Saharan
desert and showed how Algeria still held possibilities
for the courageous woman who had lost her first youth,
but retained the primitive instincts of her sex. It
was said—I know not with how much truth—that
" The Garden of Allah " and " Barbary Sheep " were
responsible for a vast number of adventurous tourists
(a large proportion of them ladies of a certain age)
taking tickets to Biskra and the borders of the Sahara.

From the selling point of view, I take it that you
found your formula useful enough. It must be
remembered that women have always been the great
novel-reading section of the community, and, which is
even more important, the great distributors of fame.
Rumour, with her thousand tongues, was justly painted
as of the female sex. And the woman of forty-odd
has ever been wont to find solace for her fading charms
in the imaginary love-affairs of others. She, above all
others, is the great dispenser of fortune to the struggling novelist ; and the man who can touch her heart
most nearly, who can persuade her that the dangerous
fascination of some women really increases rather
than deteriorates with advancing years, is assured
of success. The only trouble attendant on his good
fortune lies in the fact that publishers have an unpleasant knack of demanding that a good formula, once
found, shall be worked for something more than it is
worth. It is difficult to persuade these unimaginative
gentlemen that an artist cannot walk contentedly for
ever round the same circular track. To put Pegasus
in harness is bad enough, but it is too much to try and
turn him into a mill-horse.

The heroine of " The Call of the Blood " was also a

lady whose adventures began (somewhat to her dis-
comfiture) rather late in life. I suppose this book and
its sequel, " A Spirit in Prison," may be said to have
secured your position as a serious novelist—one of
those who can be trusted to deal with a psychological
problem with that detail and exhaustiveness that the
British public demand from a clever writer before
they consent to prepare his pedestal. It was in these
two books that I first noticed a tendency on your part
towards a distressing verbosity. " The Call of the
Blood " was kept alive by the strength of the plot, the
Sicilian setting, and the admirable character sketch of
Gaspare : in the sequel there was less material but
even more fluency. Some of us began to fear that
you had fallen in love with mere length for its own
sake, and that your future novels might outrival in
size some of the mammoths of antiquity.

In common with Mr. Eden Philpotts, a novelist of
about your own standing, both as regards age and
general reputation, you have been apt to take your
relaxation, after writing one of your more important
books, in the composition of something trifling on a
smaller scale. Thus, after " The Garden of Allah "
you published " The Black Spaniel," which is more
like an anti-vivisection tract than a novel : after " A
Spirit in Prison " came a book on Egypt and its monu-
ments and " Barbary Sheep " : between " Bella
Donna " and " The Fruitful Vine " you brought·out
a book on the Holy Land and a psychological story
called " The Dweller on the Threshold." These
intercalary works may not have always displayed you
at your best, but they possess at least the negative
merit of conciseness. We had begun to predict for
you a distinct future in the literary world. You could

write : you had abundance of ingenuity, and an eye
for a dramatic situation. Indeed, that eye may have
been too good. " Bella Donna " was dramatized—
with a success that may prove to have been her author's
ruin.

I have been re-reading during the last few days
some of your earlier works, for I always like to refresh
my memory on these points before I definitely commit
my opinion of any author to the printed page. I read
" Felix " once again, and my good opinion of the book
was confirmed : I read also " The Londoners " and
wondered what subtle quality in it that made me laugh
so consumedly in 1897 had evaporated after seven-
and-twenty years. I remember distinctly the first
time I read that story, for it was in a club library, and
on the mantelpiece of the palatial room was displayed
a placard with the word S I L E N C E inscribed
thereon in big letters. Perhaps it was just that
placard that made me choke and gurgle with dis-
simulated laughter, as one laughs hysterically at
church or during a funeral. But no ! it certainly was
funny : it was screamingly funny in parts. And yet
now I can read it soberly enough, without more than
an occasional quiet chuckle. The fact is, that farce
has to be very good indeed if it is to live. There was
a time when Jerome's " Idle Thoughts " laid the
foundation stone of a new school of British humour :
you are more likely to yawn over it now than to laugh.
And yet " Pickwick " survives. To preserve it from
decay farcical writing needs an especially large infusion
of humanity.

Mr. Max Beerbohm

Mr. Max Beerbohm

SOME irresponsible, indolent reviewer must surely before now have referred to you as the *enfant gâté* of Literature and Art. Certainly no one in my time has stormed these twin fortresses with more consummate ease, with greater *aplomb* ; in fact we are wrong to call it "storming" : the word is clearly out of place in describing your swift yet leisurely progression, each daintily shod foot planted dandiacally yet with precision on the right spot, well out of the mud. It was rare indeed for any critic to introduce a jarring note in the harmony of praise. You were acclaimed almost from the first as one of the most brilliant of living essayists. The "Yellow Book" received you gratefully upon its epicene bosom : "Pick-Me-Up" (that bright little paper that flourished in the nineties) was glad to get your caricatures of eminent gentlemen even before you had come down from Oxford : a publisher was found, in the person of the late Mr. John Lane, to collect the first sprightly runnings of your pen together in a volume under the comprehensive name of "Works." And still the critics only grinned good-humouredly. You were a privileged person, a brilliant young man, the brother of a famous actor, representative of all that was best and brightest in modern Oxford. This pose of yours was amusing—if not carried too far.   Indulgently, they let Youth have its fling.

I only remember, during all those years before the arrival of the new century, one paper setting out to " slate " you with any real severity.   That paper did not live long afterwards.   But it was your drawings rather than your literary style that roused it to a momentary frenzy.   Those early caricatures—I suppose you must have published a volume some time about 1896 or 1897—affected the editor much as Whistler's famous nocturnes affected John Ruskin. To him they were an impertinence, a schoolboy scribbling on his slate, an inkpot flung in the face of the public.   I do not suppose the diatribes of *The New Saturday*—for that was the name of this unmannerly and ill-starred periodical—caused you the least tremor of annoyance or apprehension.   You were already seated on your pinnacle.

Perennially young as you have always seemed to us oldsters, it comes as something of a shock to look you up now in " Who's Who " and find that you were born so long ago as August 24, 1872.   But then, Time foreshortens everything.   It seems only the other day that you succeeded Bernard Shaw in the dramatic critic's chair of the *Saturday Review*, and began to deal out to an expectant public a series of delightful *causeries* tacked lightly on to the plays of the preceding week.   (You note how I, too, am drawn into the prevailing chorus of praise against my will.) The fact is, yours has always been a singularly engaging personality.   Even your form master at Charterhouse —a gentleman with whom I had some slight personal acquaintance—aided and abetted you in your early literary ventures.

It is something of a coincidence, as Mr. John Lane noted in the preface to " Works," that you and Aubrey Beardsley should have chosen the same week to appear for the first time on this mundane stage. Beardsley preceded you by three days, the announcement of his birth appearing in *The Times* on the day you were born. In due course you went, like Steele and Addison and Thackeray, to Charterhouse, and thence, in 1890, to Merton, Oxford. Both at Charterhouse and Merton you are said to have started a gallery of caricatures of those in authority. And your first recorded appearance in print is to be found in *The Carthusian* of December, 1886, under the signature of Diogenes. The burden of it is a complaint against the dullness of that estimable school paper.

At Oxford you contributed to several undergraduate journals, and also made your first appearance in the new quarterly—*The Yellow Book*—which John Lane had just started. This was with " The Defence of Cosmetics," which appears in " Works " as " The Pervasion of Rouge." To the second volume of the Bodley Head publication you contributed a Letter to the Editor : to the third, " A Note on George the Fourth," together with a caricature of that amiable monarch. The " Note " received the signal honour of a parody in *Punch*.

This slight chronicle is enough to show that you had attained to a certain fame at an exceptionally early age. And some few of the essays in " Works " are surprisingly good, and even more surprisingly mature. One could have sworn that the essay on " Dandies and Dandies," which first appeared in an American magazine in 1895, had been the work of an old hand, a finished writer. Only here and there, perhaps, comes an expression that makes the reader wonder, for a moment. You were still just young enough to enjoy a sense of discovery in the use of strange words, such as " inverideed " (printed thus in a single word), or " impenuous."

In my opinion these first essays were better than those that succeeded them. You were, I suppose, no more than twenty-four years old when " Works " appeared : " More " and " Yet Again " followed, after decent intervals. You had begun early, but the booklets you permitted to appear were of no great size. You did not abuse your popularity. There came, too, one Christmas season, rendered memorable by a number of the *Saturday Review* containing some excellent parodies from your pen. I wish I could find my original copy of " A Christmas Garland."

Yes ! you have been fortunate in your reception. I do not say that your success has been altogether undeserved, but it occurs to me sometimes, as I painfully struggle along the muddy causeway, that you were caught up on high, among the Immortals, almost too early—earlier than was quite warranted by your merits. Here, for example, is " The Happy Hypocrite," illustrated in colour by a well-known artist, selling at one guinea net, and referred to in the Press as " A superb edition of a modern classic." " The Happy Hypocrite " is good stuff—but is it really as good as all that ? And then there is " Zuleika Dobson." Very well, once in a way, as a *jeu d'esprit.* . . .

You perceive that the carping spirit is beginning to grow in me. You must expect it to come, sooner or later ; and especially now that you have withdrawn yourself from London and sit remote in far Rapallo, not giving your undoubted personal charm any further opportunity of getting in its work. I like to read a few essays of yours occasionally : I like better to look throguh a few of your caricatures now and then, and to note how delicately you puncture the self-esteem of my old friends with the sharp needle of satire. (The letterpress of your caricatures is often the best thing about them.) But I do think you were the Fortunate Youth of the late nineteenth century. And I also admit that, without you, that curious period would not have been quite the same thing.

Mr. Rudyard Kipling

Mr. Rudyard Kipling

A FRIEND of mine, who knew you better than I shall ever do, once remarked that you were apt to prove a prickly companion. I do not suppose he meant any harm by this : probably all that he meant to say was that you were a strong man with the temperament of an artist. Ever since you began to write you have been accustomed to say just what you thought, as vividly and forcibly as possible ; which implies almost of necessity that you have written some things and expressed some opinions that you would like to forget, if your enemies would allow you to do so.

Most readers know by now that you were educated at the United Services College at Westward Ho !, in company with Stalky and Corkran and Mr. King and several other more or less life-like characters who still occasionally crop up when the editor of some American magazine persuades you to write another short story. To India you returned from that singular educational establishment at the age of seventeen, to become subeditor of the Lahore *Civil and Military Gazette*, and, later on, to write for the *Pioneer*. I suppose, if it had not been for defective eyesight, you would have followed the example of most of your schoolfellows and gone back to India, if at all, as a subaltern.

The spectacles of " Beetle " have a good deal to answer for. Indubitably it was a great thing that you should have returned to India at that early age, and a greater thing still (from the point of view of English Literature) that you should have gone back without an official position under the British Government. The civil servant and the military officer are alike cramped by the shackles of routine and by a wholesome fear of the authorities. For the most part they see only one side of Indian life, and that the least interesting, and they cannot even write freely about their own little section without considerable danger of offence. You were a journalist—a man whose profession it was to see as much of the life around him as possible—and you had an observant pair of eyes behind those spectacles. Through your father, then curator of the Lahore Museum, you had access to the ordinary official circles. But you were among them, not of them, and this fact gave you the power, denied to the majority of Anglo-Indians, of depicting the follies and foibles of those around you without the unpleasant after-thought that you might be suspected of treachery to your own class.

You could write, too, without that natural nervousness as to criticism that might have cramped you had you remained in England. Your first published works were volumes of stories collected from your own paper, written with all the careless and outspoken candour of youth. Undoubtedly there are some writers who are the better for being exposed to the cross-fire of the critics, but I fancy we should have lost something of the essential Kipling if you had published your first volumes at home, with the *Saturday Review* and the *Spectator* looming large before the young author's vision.

It was some time in the late eighties, 1888 or 1889, that our bookstalls in the railway stations began to display certain slim volumes, in unfamiliar wrappers of a greyish blue, bearing an author's name that many of us hastily concluded must be imaginary. Rudyard was in itself uncommon : Kipling had even a flavour of the comic : the collocation seemed obviously the happy thought of a writer determined to challenge attention at all hazards. It was not long before the name began to be heard all over the country. I remember the first volume of the series I managed to procure. It was " The Story of the Gadsbys " that introduced me to the new writer. I think I have read everything of yours that has been published since.

Now " The Story of the Gadsbys " is, most decidedly, not one of your happiest efforts. Reading it now we are inclined to stop every now and then and marvel at the success it had in those Victorian days. But I confess I was captured then. The fact is, you were the first to adopt that sort of manner. In a few months we had scores trying to imitate you. And again you opened a new world to English readers. Before you appeared on the bookstalls we knew nothing of the inner life of the great dependency that is now, apparently, trying to shake off its yoke. We had read stories of the Mutiny : some of us may have had a hazy knowledge of India's earlier history —of the days of Clive, and Warren Hastings, and the taking of Seringapatam, or the battle of Assaye. But of the inner life of India we knew practically nothing until (as Mr. H. G. Wells has poetically said) you opened in these thin grey volumes a series of " shutters to reveal the dusty sun-glare and blazing colours of the East." Nothing so vivid and actual had been written

H

for a generation. And the inevitable result followed. As is usual when a new writer springs into sudden fame, a school arose that sedulously copied the little tricks and mannerisms of the latest success, and the English language acquired a jerkiness and a fancy for sudden transition that have left their traces upon it to the present day.

Your arrival heralded the epoch of the Short Story (new style), which flourished exceedingly in this country for awhile towards the close of the nineteenth century. (There are signs of a slight revival at the present day—only the style is, of course, newer still.) But for ten years or so it really looked as though this form of art had come to stay : as though the art of Maupassant, about which the *cognoscenti* used to prate so readily, had acclimatized itself across the channel. Solemn critics began to talk learnedly about the technique of the *conte*, as they loved to call it ; young authors began to experiment ; publishers even seemed disposed to buy. But the critics, pestilent fellows, would not be satisfied until they had imposed rules for the new game, and they soon decided that the Short Story and the Anecdote were two different things. To call a short story by this name—" a mere anecdote "—became a stock term of abuse. It damped the butterfly wings of these young authors, afflicting them with a vague distress, and by degrees they crept off to explore other fields of endeavour.

It was against you in particular that the charge of anecdotism was brought, and it cannot be denied that some of your earlier stories narrated, in a detached manner that you had made your own, mere episodes. The short story of the previous generation had been merely a long story on a small scale : it is largely due to you, and to H. G. Wells, that its scope has been so much extended. But I suppose the critic had his effect upon you both, in the end : Mr. Wells gave up writing short stories, to the grief of judicious readers, and yours became decidedly longer. They have, in fact, been growing ever since.

I suppose it was owing to this charge that you wrote, in 1891, " The Light that Failed," a story that appeared in an American magazine before it appeared, with a different and more artistic ending, in book form. That a writer of your importance should have consented to mangle his work with the idea of conciliating the magazine public appeared almost criminal to some reviewers, and the book was not too well received. Besides, they had always maintained that your talent was not equal to producing a full-blown novel. " The Naulahka," written in conjunction with your brother-in-law, Mr. Wolcott Balestier, was even less successful. " Captains Courageous " and " Stalky and Co." had a mixed reception. It was not until you brought out " Kim," in 1901, that the carpers ceased.

Yet in each of these books there had been something that no other living writer could have accomplished. You always insisted on seeing things for yourself, with your own eyes. You absolutely refused to reflect the opinions of another. And all agreed that you possessed a marvellous faculty for assimilating yourself to new surroundings. It was not only that you acquired the terminology of a new world in a surprisingly short time, but that at the end of a few weeks your acquaintance with the inhabitants and their manners and customs seemed all but flawless. In " The Light that Failed " you wrote as though you had been familiar with every turn of the painter's mill.

You had, it was true, some slight connection with that world : two well-known artists, in the persons of Burne-Jones and Poynter, were your uncles by marriage. But then you appeared to know the fishing fleet on the Banks and their ways equally well, and the private soldiers of the army in India, and the native world there, as well as Simla and the most intimate details of official life. And for a time at least you displayed so remarkable an acquaintance with machinery, both marine and locomotive, that it was clear you must have been originally trained for an engineer.

Experts, of course, used to hint darkly that your information was not always so accurate as the layman imagined, but experts like saying this sort of thing, and when it came to the point the evidence they adduced did not amount to much. The outstanding fact remained that somehow you contrived to produce the impression of intimate knowledge of whatever subject you were treating. If "Kim" bears no resemblance to Indian life, as some wiseacres will tell us, we reply that it is India's fault. India ought to be like that—and we take refuge in the well-founded belief that the majority of Anglo-Indians know uncommonly little of the country they are supposed to govern.

Certain snatches of verse had been prefixed to some of the stories in " Plain Tales from the Hills " on their first appearance, by way of motto, and these may be regarded as the prelude to those " Barrack-room Ballads " which W. E. Henley soon began to publish in the *Scots Observer*. They appeared in book form in 1892, and at once divided the critics into two camps. Some condemned them outright as doggerel : others hailed them as an inspiration. " If this is not poetry," cried one ardent reviewer, " what is ? " Poetry or not, your verse had a tremendous influence in those ancient days when the shadow of Paul Kruger, no larger than a man's hand, was the only cloud on the political horizon. To us who were thrilled to the core then by that aggressive Imperialism, it is strange to read over some of the old verses again. The message that stirred us in the closing years of the last century sounds to-day, let us admit, like the rolling of stage thunder. A good deal of your poetry is dated—hopelessly dated —but there is enough left to furnish a handsome book, and one that will live. Curious it is that the simpler your inspiration the more lasting its appeal : I like best of all your poems, some of those dealing, not with Empire and the tumult of fighting, but with the quiet Sussex downs.

Some few years ago complaints used to be heard that you had practically ceased to write, or were confining yourself to children's books. Admirable indeed were the " Jungle Books," " Puck of Pook's Hill," and " Rewards and Fairies," but they did not fortunately complete your message to the world. I think myself that some of your most recent stories are also among your best. But then I am of those who like " The Village that Voted," which some critics profess to regard as a mere guffaw, loud and rather vulgar. " The Edge of the Evening," another of the more modern stories, is also one of my favourites. But I do not quarrel with others who think differently. I never cared much for " Brugglesmith," about which I have heard some rave, nor do I like (indeed, I actively dislike) that story dealing with a Sunday afternoon at a roadside station on the Southern line, in which figure an American doctor and a navvy to whom he has administered an emetic. I quite admit that **on**

occasion I find your sense of humour out of line with
my own, and when that happens it is difficult to persuade me that it is travelling the right road.   Yet
there are very few of your works that I do dislike :
there are many that I read over and over again.   To
me you are ſtill one of the brighteſt ſtars in our literary
firmament : I hope you may continue to shine there
for many years to come.

Mr. Hilaire Belloc

TIME was when we sent our literary men to Parliament and were not ashamed of it. Some sat there, like the immortal Gibbon, in the humble station of a mute : timidity was fortified by pride, and the success of their pens discouraged the trial of their voices. But the country, apparently, did not mind. They might be silent, but they were respected : now and again some pleasant sinecure was found for their behoof. And they were allowed a certain modicum of that independence so dear to literary minds. Party organization had not yet become the tyrant that aroused your wrath some twenty years ago. It was in 1906, I believe, that you took your seat for the first time, Member for Salford.

A brilliant young fellow of thirty-six you were then, with already something of a career behind you. Straight from school you went to become a driver in the 8th Regiment of French artillery : your service over, you matriculated at Balliol at the comparatively mature age of twenty-three, and secured a first in the History Schools. Almost at the same time came out your first volume—" Verses and Sonnets "—and a year later that really excellent little work, " The Bad Child's Book of Beasts." It certainly was not long before you got into your stride.

The world, even then, was very wicked. With your friend Chesterton, not yet converted to Popery (I must ask you to excuse these old-fashioned phrases), you resolved to essay the Herculean task of setting it right. Your method was indubitably the more subtle of the two. You were outwardly quiet, restrained, a trifle sardonic, while Mr. Chesterton gambolled around his victims like some highly accomplished and playful porpoise. I do not know which of you, in those rosy opening days of the twentieth century, produced the greater effect. Perhaps neither of you accomplished quite as much as had been hoped. The trouble with the ironic method is that the foolish are apt to take it literally—as the late Samuel Butler so often found to his cost. But the crusaders reaped some reward. Belloc and Chesterton were seen to be steadily climbing the ladder of fame side by side.

I am inclined to be sorry that you ever meddled with politics at all. I do not think Parliamentary life suits the literary man of to-day. Macaulay and Disraeli, John Stuart Mill, and (shall we say ?) Samuel Warren contrived to combine the practise of literature with life in the House of Commons : modern writers have found the conjunction more difficult to manage. Mr. A. E. W. Mason, I believe, was one of your contemporaries, but it was not long before he found the strain too much for him, and sought retirement. You were made of sterner stuff. It is possible that you might be sitting still, had not your constituents basely deserted you. But I doubt whether the experience has proved of any great advantage to you since. Politics may be fascinating, from the outside ; but there is too much rancour and bitterness about the game for my taste, and I like your work best when you are writing in a kindly and urbane spirit.

The fact is, there is quite gall enough in your writing without the continuous irritations of working under a Party System to stimulate its secretion. I notice that you have always had a tendency to follow up a season of comparative mild writing by something more than commonly malicious. Thus, in 1903, did " Caliban's Guide to Letters " succeed " The Path to Rome " and, eight years later, " The Girondin " was succeeded by " More Peers " and " The Party System." " Caliban," I allow, was sufficiently amusing, so was the story of Mr. Emanuel Burden and the tale of Mr. Clutterbuck's election, but it was also very bitter. You pursued Mr. Kipling's poetry in that book with a deadly malignancy. I confess I could never discover why you nourished so poisonous a hatred for the author of " The Recessional," but clearly there was something about him that aroused your worst feelings.

There was a lack of sympathy about you in those early farcical novels, designed to castigate hypocrisy. They remind me of Swift. I never find in them a single character for whom it is possible to feel the slightest affection or respect ; and it is only too clear that you have nothing but a whole-souled contempt for the unhappy puppets you dangle before the eyes of your readers. Like so many of these brilliant Balliol men, you are perhaps too generally contemptuous of your fellow-men. You despise the peerage, and politicians in general : you both despise and hate the Jews ; and you introduced into these books of yours characters drawn from all these sources for the mere purpose of expressing this contempt and dislike.

I think the most violent of those satirical romances was called " Pongo and the Bull "—a work which I have some recollection of reviewing when it came out, though I cannot discover it in the list of your publications to-day. You were then, I suppose, especially bitter about politics, and you drew a long, listless, invertebrate Premier who was meant to represent the Mr. Balfour of that day, and a stumpy, ape-like Leader of the Opposition, presumably intended as a caricature of the late Sir Henry Campbell-Bannerman. It is likely enough that upon a close acquaintance the leaders of great parties in the State lose something of their glamour, but you made them too idiotic to be convincing. Their talk was foolish, their actions insane, their party tactics eminently discreditable. And round about these two protagonists gibbered a crowd of maniacs hardly less astonishing—an absurd American millionaire with a mania for collecting worthless relics of Lord Beaconsfield among them. I have no objection to a farce, but this was a farce flavoured too bitterly to be amusing.

In all these satires of yours there is cleverness enough and to spare. Innumerable stinging shafts are aimed at the financier, the politician, the Jew, and at the middle classes of England, who are their contented dupes. They tend to fail of their full effect for their very number : there is no kindly, sensible fellow to act as a foil to these rapacious rogues on the one hand, these fatuous fools on the other. And your ironic method in dealing with these characters affects me unpleasantly. It is almost like a sort of treachery. You are so scrupulously polite to the unfortunate men, loading them with exaggerated compliment, while all the time you are winking behind their backs at the reader, bidding him observe what a crowd of imbecile scoundrels are these rulers of his country.

"The Girondin" was first published in 1911. So the old copy tells me which I have taken down from my shelves. I have kept the book, and every now and then I read it—which shows clearly enough the sort of opinion I have of your one romantic novel. It is a very fine book, and an individual book : no other writer that I know could have done it, or would have done it if he could, in just that way. And yet there is a shadow hanging over it all the time —a sort of hopelessness. The Revolution has come, and many things have to happen before the world can go on again in the old peaceful, happy way. But how excellent are the adventures of young Georges Boutroux, from his double duel with the two sentries guarding his uncle's house to the moment when, lying all broken in his hospital bed, his mind goes dreaming back to the girl Joyeuse and that short but exquisite romance in the woods.

I should be glad to have another novel of this kind from you. But it is improbable that I shall. The fact is, you are almost too variously gifted. A poet, and a considerable poet, you have written at least two things that will outlast our little day. Of its kind, "The Path to Rome" is the best book I know since the days of R. L. Stevenson. You have collected three or four volumes of essays : you are a publicist and journalist of sufficient standing, and during the war you encouraged the pessimists week by week in the columns of *Land and Water*. You should have had a K.B.E. at least for those services

—but honours seldom fall upon the right head.   In
these days I rarely see your name on the title-page
of a new book, and there is something jejune about
the essays you occasionally contribute to the press.
They are combative, but you seem able to find nothing
really worthy of your steel.   I take it you will always
be combative ;   like most stalwart fighters you will
probably never settle down comfortably in a world so
manifestly imperfect.

Mr. Morley Roberts

Mr. Morley Roberts

THERE are authors in every generation who are more favourably known to those of their own craft than to the public, who have a reputation in literary circles but are little considered by the layman. For some reason or other, sometimes very difficult to discover, they have never had a real popular success. It is easy enough to determine (or to invent) a reason for the success of an author when it has arrived ; but it is altogether a different matter to try and discover why a mass of work in various forms, some of it really excellent in quality and all of it commanding the respect due to artistic workmanship, should have been so poorly received. I have had a guess now and then with regard to isolated specimens of your work, but I have never been able to fathom the mystery entirely.

It is perilously near thirty years now since I first became acquainted with you. Your wanderings were over then—at any rate for a time—and you had settled down to the business of writing novels and short stories, with occasional excursions into journalism. When you first began to think of writing I cannot say, but you had served the right sort of apprenticeship for one who means to deal in Romance. I remember very well the first time I saw your photograph reproduced.

I

It was in a copy of *The Idler*, then run, I think, by
Jerome K. Jerome and Robert Barr, to whom had
occurred the happy thought of a series of articles on
" How I Began to Write " by Some Who had Done It.
(I don't suppose that was the actual name of the series,
but it is as near as I can get to it after all these years.)
All the young writers of that time contributed—
Stevenson, and Conan Doyle, and Anthony Hope, I
suppose, and yourself—and my recollection of you is
that some at least of your photographs with which the
article was illustrated represented you in cow-boy
costume. A handsome-looking young fellow you were
then, too. And the article itself gave particulars of
some of the adventures you had already been through.
I wish I had kept that article : I read it with a certain
envy. How easy must the writing of stories be to a
man who had your experience ! Bear in mind that I
was young then myself, and very new to the business
of writing.

I do not know that you have changed very much, in
manner or appearance, since the nineties. Certainly
you do not look your age. Yet it is a fact that you
went to Australia and were working on Victorian
railroads and stock-riding in New South Wales while
I was still a small boy at a preparatory school. And
you had served before the mast by then, I suppose, on
the *Essex*. It was later—perhaps when I was at Winchester or Cambridge—that you worked your way
round the greater part of North America, trying your
hand at saw-mills and railroads, sheep and cattle, from
Texas and California up to Manitoba and British
Columbia. I believe you may claim to have helped in
the construction of the C.P.R. And since those days
of my early and your own comparative youth you have

been away occasionally for a matter of half a year or so visiting such parts of the world as you had been compelled to overlook before—the Cape and Rhodesia and the Transvaal (in the days of Paul Kruger, with whom you recorded an interview), the South Seas and Central America with the West Indies (whither you are travelling, I believe, at the moment of my writing these words). Certainly you have done more unceremonious knocking about the world than most of your brother authors.

" The Western Avernus " was your first book, and it dates from 1887, the Year of Jubilee. A book of experiences, this, and very well received, for it was something new in those days and unusual for a writer to be quite frank about such matters as walking the streets of San Francisco without money enough to get a meal. " The Western Avernus " did quite well, and has been re-issued more than once since : it deserves to live.

Then you began the heart-breaking job of writing short stories for a living. One of these days, I suppose, some critic of importance will awake to the fact that you have had a very considerable influence on this form of art in England, and will produce a long and probably quite unreadable treatise on the subject, too late to do you any good. The fact is, you were one of the leaders of the new movement that started in the early nineties after the rise of Rudyard Kipling. For a short time there was a cult, a school of modern English short story-writers. Kipling himself, Barrie and Stevenson, Henry James and Arthur Morrison, Pett Ridge and W. W. Jacobs, George Gissing and H. G. Wells were all employing this form. Several out of this list are fortunately still alive, but not many continue faithful to the short story. You and W. W. Jacobs, with Pett

Ridge lending very occasionally a helping hand, appear to be the only survivors capable of dealing with the editor of a modern magazine.

Many of your sea stories are as good as anything of the kind I know : some of your stories of the Wild West —Texas and Arizona—come in a good second ; but I am inclined to think that your Canadian and British Columbian stories strike a more individual note than either.   I am not going to ferret about in my books for the purpose of extracting my favourite specimens : the generous student can buy a collection for himself if he wishes to compare and criticise.   For it is true that you have written a considerable number of books. I do not actually know the number, but I know that the list given in the books of reference is altogether incomplete.   I have myself a whole shelf in my library filled with nothing but Roberts, and a second is already making a promising start.   Probably you have topped eighty volumes by now : perhaps you are over the hundred mark : I cannot tell.   But I expect I know the body of your work better than any other critic now living outside your own family.

" Maurice Quain," published in 1897, was the first of your novels to come into my hands.   That must have been shortly after I first played a game of chess with you at the old Authors' Club in Whitehall Court —a club of which I believe you are still an ornament now that it has died and been born again.   In those days it is hardly too much to say that you *were* the Authors' Club.   Your spirit pervaded the place : your voice was commonly audible as soon as the door of the smoking-room was opened.   But I must not be led into talking of the Club : it is with your novels that I am now concerned.

You have written perhaps half a dozen novels that are worthy of careful consideration when the critics come to sum up English fiction during the last half-century. And the most successful of them all (which, curiously enough, happened to be also the best) may perhaps have sold something like five thousand copies. Your novel-writing, in effect, has not been really a pay-ing proposition. This sort of thing cannot be helped, and it is no good waxing indignant and pointing scorn-fully to the authors who have sold forty, fifty or a hundred thousand copies of infinitely inferior books. Indubitably your novels lacked some ingredient that makes for popularity, and I do not suppose that now, after all these years, they are ever likely to com-mand a big sale. But the reading public may have my sincere assurance that some of them are Literature. Equally candidly I assure them that some are diffi-cult, irritating, unpleasantly violent. It has happened to you occasionally, as it has happened to greater artists, to be compelled to write something in a hurry and sell it to a publisher for what it will fetch, rather than find yourself cast out into the cold streets without food or clothing. In short, you have sometimes written " pot-boilers," as they are called in artistic circles. I do not say that your " pot-boilers," whether short stories or long, are unreadable. Most of your stuff is readable : is even worth reading ; but there is sometimes a sort of extravagant flippancy about your manner that is curiously unamusing. I mistrust you especially when you openly declare your intention of being " joyous."

Yet I admit that you did at least one flippant book as well as need be—perhaps as well as it could be done in that particular fashion. This was a little book,

published, I think, by Sands & Co. in 1900, and called
" The Descent of the Duchess."   But then it was so
small a book as to be barely distinguishable from a short
story.   The idea was novel, and no time was wasted :
we were not allowed to get tired of the situation.   In
their own way, some of these " long short stories "
are the most successful things you have done : I recall
another, also originally published in book form, called
" A Sea Comedy," which could hardly have been
bettered.   But, good as these are, no critic is likely to
pretend that they are the most important part of your
literary work.

" Rachel Marr " is undoubtedly the finest book you
ever wrote.   And it is really a great novel—a novel
that anyone might have been proud to sign.   If the
reader has not yet seen it he can congratulate himself
on having a literary treat in store.   I do not know
any other writer who could have done the book in the
same way—who could have pitched it from the start
in so lofty a key and kept it at that pitch right through
to the end.   (I do not say that the reader will like the
book—that is altogether a different matter—but if
he has any judgment he will be forced to confess that
it is a literary masterpiece.)

" David Bran " came a little later, but I do not think
it attracted so much attention.   Yet this was also a fine
novel.   I should be inclined to place it second in order
of merit.   And after it I should rank " The Flying
Cloud," in which you put all your love and knowledge
of the sea, and " Time and Thomas Waring," which
shows you in yet another light as, shall we say, an
amateur of the operating theatre.   But there are a
host of other books that seem to demand notice—
" Henry Maitland," for example, which aroused a lot

of controversy when it came out, a year or two before
the war, and " The Colossus," which dealt, as you might
expect, with Cecil Rhodes, " and " Lord Linlithgow,"
which " featured " another famous politician, and
" The Prey of the Strongest," the scene of which is a
saw-mill in British Columbia. (An admirable piece of
work, that, palpitating with life.) Well ! I am not
going to make a catalogue. I shall name no more of
your novels.

But you possess a restless brain, still thirsting for
new worlds to conquer. I spoke just now of " Time
and Thomas Waring," in which you start off, boldly
and characteristically, with an opening sentence that
could hardly fail to send a shiver through a nervous
reader. I must give it :—

> The operating theatre was lighted from the north end by a large
> window which was also partly a skylight. Under the window stood
> radiators. The chief aspect of the place was one of intense and scrupu-
> lous cleanliness. The walls were of white and gleaming tiles : bright
> metal work glittered. On the left there were standing basins of white
> ware against the wall. The floor was of a close grey concrete. Near
> the standing basins there was a brass structure. By this were boilers
> of nickel with cold and hot sterilized water in them. To the right
> was a glass cupboard with shining instruments in it. Above it in the
> wall an electric fan was running.

From the point of view of the circulating library I
can hardly imagine a much worse beginning. But the
fact is, you were already beginning to take what I can
only term an unhealthy interest in surgery. I do not
know how many operations, major and minor, you
have undergone since I first met you, but it has always
seemed to me that you announced each new impending
visit to a nursing home with a sort of melancholy
pride. It was another sort of experience, after all :

one of these days this also would have its use.   And
by degrees you became our chief authority at the club
on all manner of disease and the triumphs of modern
surgery.   I believe for a short while you wondered
whether it were really too late for you to go through a
medical course, take a degree, and start carving your
fellow creatures physically after dissecting them spirit-
ually for so many years.   In default of that you could
—and did—write books on medical science.

They tell me you are now a recognized light in
circles where move the consulting physician, the
knighted surgeon.   At the sight of your typescript the
Lancet inclines a stately head, the *B.M.J.* (I suppose
these journals still exist) displays a momentary liveliness.   You write of such matters as " Warfare in
the Human Body " and so forth—which interest me
not at all, or only when I have reason to fear that my
own carcase is likely to become the theatre of operations.   But it reflects a certain subdued glory also
upon ourselves, when a mere layman, uncertificated
like the rest of us, is tacitly admitted within the magic
circle.

Whatever subject you chose to attack you would
startle, if I know anything of you.   And what a
number of different trades you must have tried, in your
time !   Certainly there are few sorts of writing that
you have neglected—you were once even a writer in
the India Office.   Perhaps, after all, Nature intended
you for a biographer.   The " W. H. Hudson, A
Portrait " which Messrs. Nash and Grayson published
about a year ago, is perhaps as fine a piece of work as
you have yet done.

Mr. William Babington Maxwell

Mr. William Babington Maxwell

VERY few novelists have had the fortune to spring from the union of a publisher with one of the best sellers of his time. I take it you must have felt, from your first youth, that the career of a novelist was marked out for you, that it would be a species of impiety to do anything but follow in the footsteps of the charming writer who entranced our youthful days with " Lady Audley's Secret " and " Vixen." (I recollect falling hopelessly in love with the heroine of " Vixen " at an early age.) Genius is not often handed down in unbroken succession, but there is ground for supposing that some fraction of your present success may be due to the talented lady who used to write under the name of Miss M. E. Braddon. As to the publishing side of your parentage, it would surely have been sinful to neglect a connection with such a firm as Hurst and Blackett, which, I believe, succeeded to Mr. Maxwell's business.

At the moment I cannot recall many instances of famous woman writers being rivalled, or even eclipsed, by the glory of their sons. There was, in the past, Anthony Trollope: to-day we have Mr Gilbert Frankau and yourself : midway between the two the late Major Hesketh Prichard used to collaborate with his mother in fiction—an unusual combination. It has been more common to find daughters (as with Thackeray and Charles Kingsley) carrying on the tradition of the house. But those who knew Miss Braddon intimately never ceased to be aſtonished at the amount of time she could find in a busy life to help all those around her. I take it she taught you a good deal of your craft. The careful observer can trace her influence in almoſt every book you have written.

Nevertheless, with all these advantages, you did not rush into print with any indecent haſte. The firſt work credited to you in books of reference is " The Countess of Maybury," which did not appear until 1901, at which time you and I were both about thirty-five years old. The Countess belonged to her age : she was a more foolish relation of Mr. Benson's " Dodo," and had some affinities with the airy chatterers who appeared in the " Dolly Dialogues " of the present Sir Anthony Hope Hawkins. Then came a book of short ſtories, and then, in 1904, a more serious and important work—" The Ragged Messenger." A very good book too. Careful critics, no doubt, placed a secret mark againſt your name after reading it, noting your previous hiſtory. One of these days, said they, you would indubitably arrive. Anxious not to disappoint them, you wrote " The Guarded Flame " two years later. It remains, I consider, the beſt book you have yet done—very possibly the beſt you will ever do.

Before " The Guarded Flame," however, you wrote " Vivien," which gave you a comfortable position at the libraries among the great mass of incurably sentimental readers. These two books, it seems to me, give us considerable insight into the nature of their gifted author. I have always maintained that you possess a double personality. In these two early books you showed them to us quite clearly, separate : in later works we are often privileged to watch the two Maxwells struggling for the mastery.

Yes, there are two of you, and one is a legacy from your mother. By birth and training you are a Victorian, but the Spirit of the Age does its best to fit you for the book-shelves of the present day. " Vivien," of course, was an excellent specimen of sound, old-fashioned work. I remember that when I first read the book I came to the conclusion that you had decided, in a jesting spirit, to take that oldest of all themes —the nobleman and the poor governess—and demonstrate how engrossing a story might still be woven out of the old material. There was not an ounce of psychology in the whole book. But, if you were really trying an experiment, it was abundantly justified. The old story held its readers as well as ever. In places the more sophisticated may have smiled, for the young duke was so very ducal and all the machinery so obviously belonged to the good old type. But the true romantic closed the book at the end with a sigh of content that the heroine had arrived safe in port after her many troubles. She felt that she had obtained good emotional value for her money.

But how entirely different was " The Guarded Flame " ! No cloying sentiment about that. There you showed how, at need, you could psychologize with the best of the moderns. When it came to exposing a certain type of character you could be as clever and as merciless as any of them. And at the same time you retained that thorough-going Victorian spirit of yours. When you had a big scene you never shirked it : you set it out, on the contrary, for all you were worth : you squeezed the last drop out of your emotional lemon. It is, as I regretfully realize, the Only Way. After all, the novelist is out to excite emotion : it is his job : the public expect it of him, as they expect a certain amount of pain when they visit a dentist. The more hardy of spirit have been known to express disappointment at feeling nothing when persuaded to take gas.

Then there was " Mrs. Thompson," which displayed the two Maxwells making some attempt towards fusion. Here, again, we have something of an experiment. In this novel you take for your heroine a woman already elderly, a widow with a grown-up daughter, who has rescued from ruin the moribund shop left by her first husband and developed it into a big department store that is the pride and wonder of Mallingbridge. The opening of the story discovers this estimable lady at the height of her prosperity, rather stout, rather foolishly devoted to her anæmic daughter—in short, anything but the customary heroine of romance. Elderly women were just beginning to find themselves moved forward into the limelight at that time, for Mr. Hichens had discovered the vast reserves of romantic passion that still surge in the bosoms of mature ladies tottering on the verge of fifty. But to make Mrs. Thompson at once an elderly widow, and a shop-keeper, was decidedly a bold stroke. Yet you certainly contrived to make of her an arresting figure.

Here again, when she has to go through the mill, you see to it that she goes through it thoroughly. She permits her idolized daughter to be carried off by one idle scamp, and yields herself to another, an even greater scoundrel, under whose destructive hand

the great and glorious house of Thompson is slowly
humbled to the dust. The shadow of impending
ruin looms darkly over everything, like an immense,
growing thunder-cloud. And then, suddenly, comes
a flash—and we see our way out—an almost too ingenious way, perhaps too completely successful for a
novel. I remember an acutely critical friend com-
plaining to me that the book was a short story spoiled.
But it was a good example of the two Maxwells beginning to work in conjunction.

The next year came " In Cotton Wool " and
" General Mallock's Shadow "—the one a depressing
study in psychology and the other a story that would
have been very much on the same lines had not your
second self taken the matter in hand and decided
to supply a happy ending. Here the curious may
observe Maxwell the mind-dissector and Maxwell
the universal provider of sentimental felicity almost
quarrelling over their respective shares in the business.

Then came " The Devil's Garden," which appeared
just before the war, and was banned by the libraries,
with the usual pleasing effect on the author's reputation and sales. For a time you went soldiering in the
Royal Fusiliers. Since you came back I have seen at
least three more of your stories. I reviewed one
only the other day. " Elaine at the Gates " was its
rather remarkable name. Not a particularly good
Maxwell, but interesting to the student, because the
double personality of the author is as clearly visible as
ever. The Victorian side is perhaps now a trifle
subdued : it peeps out almost by stealth, as though
you were slightly ashamed of this tendency to romantic
sentiment that time has hitherto been unable to
quench. The Georgian Maxwell, on the other hand,

is rather pleased with himself. I gather that he enjoys showing us all how modern he really is. The name of Freud is familiar to him, and he is quite well up in post-war slang as employed by young ladies of the louder type ; nor does he hesitate for a moment to deal in the frankest manner with subjects from which our grandmothers would have recoiled blushing in affright. Sometimes, I fancy, he leads you almost too far, so absorbed does he become in the study of a new character. There is, for instance, one Mark Awdrey in this book, one of the best modern clergymen I have met in fiction. Admirably observed— but how he must have annoyed your Victorian side !

I doubt sometimes whether you will ever do anything again quite so good as " The Guarded Flame." But I suppose we are not yet too old, you and I, to produce our best work. I am inclined to think you have never succeeded altogether so far in fusing your two component parts into one great and glorious whole. If and when you do, we may have something from you more than worthy of your distinguished ancestry.

NO. XV

Mr. David Herbert Lawrence

Mr. David Herbert Lawrence

IT is true that I cannot lay claim to have made an exhaustive study of the collected works of Mr. D. H. Lawrence. With the best will in the world even a reviewer cannot hope to keep pace with all our newest prophets ; he must select from the crowd, and his selection must almost necessarily be conditioned by his personal likes and dislikes. It is probable that I should have sedulously avoided the author with whom I am dealing just now after the first two volumes of his that I had chanced to read, had I not happened upon a third one afternoon at the club when there was nothing doing in the way of bridge or billiards. I sat down to read—possibly in something of a hostile spirit, for my previous researches in the Laurentian park had not inclined me to like the proprietor, and it had always seemed to me that certain critics had entered into an informal agreement to hold him up as a Great Writer of English. Hitherto I had seen no signs of great writing. Like most of my tribe, I suppose I am easily put off by a suspicion of over-praise. I decided that Lawrence was only one more of those numerous writers who have the good or evil fortune to become the pets of a certain côterie. There is generally something unpleasant about their work—something that makes it a little difficult for the ordinary person to appreciate their excellence.

That, naturally, is where the Critic comes in. The discerning eye perceives the spark of genius glowing faintly beneath the superincumbent mass, and is confident that with the breath of his applause he can fan it into a steady flame. It is true that in order to accomplish this he has to get his nose rather close to the rubbish heap. But, after all, the discovery of a new genius is not a thing that is likely to happen oftener than once a month or so. It is worth while to take a few risks.

The first book by this new prodigy that I happened to see was not, perhaps, a favourable specimen. It was called " Aaron's Rod," and it seemed to me to have no merit whatsoever. Then, not so very long ago, chance brought me a volume of short stories to review, called " England, My England." I cannot pretend even now, with my greater knowledge of the author's mental processes, to guess why he chose this title for this particular book. I had a suspicion—very possibly quite unfounded—that he selected it by way of a jest, hoping perhaps that some sturdy but unimaginative patriot of the old school might thereby be lured into buying a copy, possibly as a gift-book for his son (aged fifteen). And it really would have been rather comic when the old fellow sat down to sample the goods, just to make certain that the sentiment was thoroughly sound. I wonder how long it would be before our sturdy squire hurled the volume violently into the fire-place.

The fact is, this collection of short stories is a pathological affair. A private sanatorium, through which the visitor is graciously allowed to stroll on payment of a moderate fee, making what he can of the inmates. In every section he will find at least one patient afflicted with some form of the disease that is our specialist's chief concern. There are some, I suppose, who enjoy this morbid atmosphere. Personally, I hate morbidity, in every form. I dislike the faint air of unwholesomeness, like some sickly scent, that seems to hang about all Lawrence's work. No doubt he would put it down to some latent antagonism—he is great on latent antagonisms—between the creator and the recipient : I prefer to explain it by assuming that there is a kink somewhere in his mind, whereas my own is almost painfully sane.

This aggressive sanity, it may be remarked, has always stood in the way of my advancement in the world of letters. Your modern critic will never quite believe in you unless you display unequivocal signs of mental aberration.

It was some time afterwards that I chanced upon " The Ladybird."

" The Ladybird " is a volume containing three stories, which are certainly altogether unlike any other short stories that we see collected in volumes or, indeed, in any form. And I approached this book with a distinct prejudice against the author, for I read on the wrapper the pronouncement of some journalistic critic that each of the stories therein contained was separately a masterpiece. Also, a little further on, I saw that " Aaron's Rod " was the most important thing that had happened in English Literature since the war. . . . To read it was to drink of a fountain of life. Now I had read " Aaron's Rod " and I had not felt in the least as though I had been drinking from any fountain whatsoever ; my impression was that I had incautiously taken a draught from some stagnant pool surrounded by a manure heap.

But I readily admit that these stories have singular merit. They seem always trying to express something difficult, if not impossible, of comprehension ; but they are full of strange and subtle analogies, and extraordinarily well done. They present certain pictures that haunt the memory, like that of Count Dionys Psanek lying on his hospital bed in the opening story, visited by Lady Daphne and her mother, or that other of the two women who are trying to run the farm in " The Fox," and the boy soldier who stumbles in on them so unexpectedly and stays. Lawrence's men are commonly possessed of a curious latent quality, something inexplicable that piques the curiosity of women and results eventually in their capture or submission. In fact, he favours the Egyptian sphinx rather than the Greek. With him the male is the enigmatic sex.

I think " The Captain's Doll " is perhaps the most satisfactory of the three stories collected in this volume. But all three are decidedly not to be labelled as negligible. They made me resolve to read more Lawrence when I found an opportunity. I did not altogether like his stories, but I could not help seeing that they had their good points. There was, for example, that wonderful description of the expedition up the mountain in the story I have mentioned. The man could write, and he had originality : most certainly these were not specimens of customary fiction. In each one of them he was trying to say something—something that was very difficult. It may not have been worth saying, but that is another matter.

Presumably most of these books have been written with the intention (borrowed from Nietzsche) of disturbing our complacency. I suppose he thinks that this England of ours is still far too comfortable, too much sunk in easy slothfulness of mind—even since the war came to wake us up. Or it may be because of the war : we are corrupted by those old cardinal virtues (as we used to esteem them), by sympathy and kindliness and humanity ; they have descended upon us as a sort of reaction from that sullen anger that so many of his male characters possess, and seem to cherish with his approval. Lawrence apparently would have us all cast aside this altruistic nonsense and worship Selfishness. Not otherwise shall we ever learn to feel clearly or will strongly.

A singular gospel, with which my instincts are wholly at variance.

And then I read " Kangaroo " and " The Boy in the Bush "—two Australian stories, one of which you wrote (for it is time I addressed a few words to you personally) in collaboration with M. L. Skinner. In this, too, I notice, you take occasion to speak of the " unplumbed crater of silent anger that lay at the bottom of his soul." Your young hero, Jack Grant, possesses " an indifference which was really congealed anger, and which gave him a kind of innocent, remote, child-like quietness." Jack Grant's first impression of Australia was that the place would be all right if it were not for the people. And especially the women. This sex antagonism is always cropping up in your works. Jack himself " hated women. He hated the kind of nausea he felt after they had crowded in upon him." He hated their eyes—Monica's eyes, which were yellow cat-eyes, and Mary's, which were like pools of ink. And Grace's big nose, and Aunt Matilda's red hair and gold chains. There is almost always something inexplicable about these eyes of yours. In "Kangaroo" you have Callcott, looking at Somers with glowing, smiling eyes which the other man could not quite understand, "eyes with something desirous, and something perhaps fanatical in them." And then Cooley, the "Kangaroo" himself, with his dark, subtle, equivocal eyes.

These are both strange, amorphous books, into which you have crowded as much of your thoughts about things in general (loosely connected with Australia) as a man well can. And I am not going to say that some of the thoughts were not worth stating. Most of them were. But many were so difficult to state that they seemed to baffle you ; you could only fly round them in narrowing circles. Yet out of the two books, vaguely, we get a curiously intimate picture of Australia. There is Sydney with its outskirts, gradually degenerating into wide sandy roads dotted with small bungalows, beyond the backs of which lay a whole aura of rusty tin cans chucked out over the back fence. In the other book it is Western Australia and farming life in the bush. Here is a characteristic passage :

> The bush was now full of sparks of the beautiful, uncanny flowers of Western Australia, and bright birds started and flew. Sombre the bush was in itself, but out of the heavy dullness came sharp, scarlet, flame-spark flowers, and flowers as lambent gold as sunset, and wan, white flowers, and flowers of a strange, darkish rich blue, like the vault of heaven just after sundown.

There is poetry in this, and also that characteristic vagueness, as of a man groping after something that

he cannot quite find. Also you display a certain
fondness for repetition. Look at the way you play
upon "flowers" here, and the idea of flame and
sparks. I find the same thing again towards the end
of the same book, in your description of Hilda Bless-
ington, whom Jack meets under rather embarrassing
circumstances and, we are rather led to believe, persuades in the end to come and live with Monica and
himself.

> There was something slightly uncanny about her, her quick, rabbit-
> like alertness and her quick, open defiance, like some unyielding animal.
> She was more like a hare than a rabbit : like a she-hare that will fight
> all the cats that are after her young. And she had a great capacity for
> remaining silent and remote, like a quaint rabbit unmoving in a corner.

"The Boy in the Bush," up to the moment when
Jack kills his rival, struck me as better than anything
of yours I had read. After that it seemed to lose
itself in a maze of analysis. And about it, as about
most of your other books, there was discernible,
through the flowers and the eau-de-cologne, an unpleasant stench, as in the Kangaroo's room after he
had been shot through the marsupial pouch, to use
his own expression.

If I had not read, afterwards, "Sons and Lovers,"
it is possible I might have left you on this note, still
rather wondering how you could have aroused the
enthusiasm among some eminent critics that at first
surprised and rather irritated me. But "Sons and
Lovers" is a fine book. I think it is the finest novel
I have read for the last ten years It has character
in it, and largeness of conception, and passages of
real beauty. And, for once in a way, there is not
much in it that I would have omitted. But I confess

I wonder how, after writing the story of the two Morels and their family, you could have produced some of the stuff that you have published since. So far, it seems to me, " Sons and Lovers " remains incomparably your best work. If you can do any more nearly as good as that, the sooner you bring them out the better for your reputation.

Mr. John Masefield

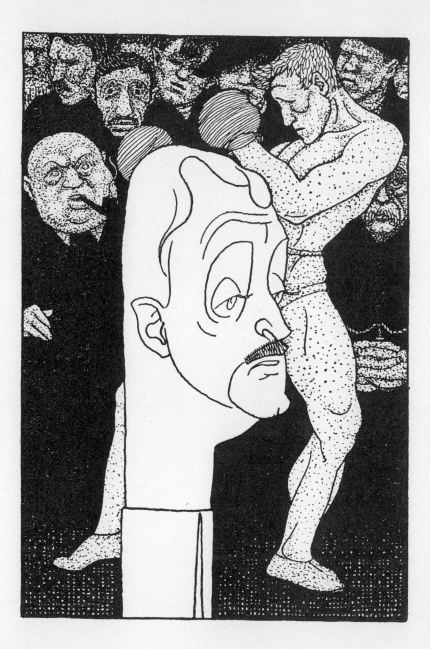

Mr. John Masefield

I DO not know much about your history, for you are one of the reticent few who conceal from the curious inquirer even such trifles as the date and place of birth. But I have read at different times a good deal of your poetry, and not a little of your prose, and I have seldom seen anything of yours that was not worth reading. Which, in these days of " free verse " and other strange ebullitions of the poetic spirit, is to say a good deal.

I will assume that you are in early middle age, like most of us, without laying too much emphasis upon the early part of it. It is pretty clear that you have been to sea in the merchant service, probably as an apprentice in a sailing ship, and I should judge that you have knocked about the world a good deal in various capacities since. That, however, is not my chief concern. Experience of out-of-the-way places is an excellent thing for the writer. And I notice that you call yourself a writer—not a poet, nor a novelist, nor even a play-wright, but just a writer.

Yet you are a poet, indubitably. A poet of the new order, perhaps, owing little enough to tradition. You have always been more concerned with matter than with manner, with what you had to say rather

than the phrasing of it. And your early life made
you, naturally enough, a thought impatient with those
who had never known what it meant to be really " up
against it." My literary friends who have served
before the mast sometimes try manfully to conceal
their just contempt for us who have done nothing of
the kind, but they find it very difficult. What can
we really know about anything unless we have suffered
as they have suffered ? You are perhaps too apt to
lay all the stress upon mere physical torture. You
are all for the ranker, the common sailor-man up aloft
in a Cape Horner rather than the skipper down below
on the quarter-deck. You are jealous of authority.
In the " Consecration " prefixed to your book of collected verse you put down your preferences clearly :

> Not of the princes and prelates with periwigged charioteers
> Riding triumphantly laurelled to lap the fat of the years

do you choose to sing, but rather

> The men of the tattered battalion which fights till it dies,
> Dazed with the dust of the battle, the din and the cries,
> The men with the broken heads and the blood running into
>   their eyes.

And again, in a single verse,

> Not the bemedalled Commander, beloved of the throne,
> Riding cock-horse to parade when the bugles are blown
> But the lads who carried the koppie and cannot be known.

One may deduce from this that you are no out-
and-out admirer of the gilded and decorated staff,
and, further, that you intend to speak out plainly what
you mean regardless of the conventions that used to
insist on what was sometimes called " poetical " lan-

guage.   The poets of our youth would never have written that line

> . . . the broken heads and the blood running into their eyes.

They would have dressed it up somehow so that we should not meet it in all its nakedness.   Nor would their commander have ridden " cock-horse " to parade, nor would they have spoken of a " koppie." " Kopje " perhaps—if they were writing soon after the Boer War.   But Masefield's muse has nothing of the dressmaker about her.   If we pronounce the thing like that we'll spell it like that, without pretence.

It may be admitted that, in your earlier poems, you carried realism rather far in places.   Your " Salt-Water Ballads," I imagine, were more or less inspired by Kipling's barrack-room verses, but they were even more unrestrained in the violence of their language. In " The Yarn of the *Loch Achray* " we come across three " bloodys " and two " blushings " (which presumably amount to the same thing, a trifle more delicately expressed) in ten stanzas.   I do not think this record is surpassed elsewhere.   But this does not prevent most of the verses from being very good indeed.

The sea haunted you, as it haunts so many who have served it.   There are passages scattered here and there among your poems that witness to its power. Take   Sea-Fever " :

> I must down to the seas again, to the lonely sea and the sky,
> And all I ask is a tall ship and a star to steer her by,
> And the wheel's kick and the wind's song and the white sail's
>   shaking,
> And a grey mist on the sea's face and a grey dawn breaking.

Or this again from " The Buccaneer " :

> There's a sea-way somewhere where all day long
> Is the hushed susurrus of the sea,
> The mewing of the skuas and the sailor's song
> And the wind's cry calling me.

In this first volume of yours there is a good deal
that is clearly derivative. " Vagabond " recalls " For
to Admire " in Kipling's " Seven Seas."   But before
long you struck out a line of your own, something
that was old enough to be almost new again.   The
long narrative poem had not received much attention
of recent years, since the death of John Davidson.
Modern readers of verse did not seem to possess the
healthy appetite of their forefathers, and it had almost
become a canon of the amateur critic that a long poem
was a contradiction in terms.   It was left to you to
revive this form of verse, and to set upon it your own
seal.   Nobody had ever done it in precisely this
manner before.   Here and there we may think we
perceive an echo—a touch of Crabbe, perhaps, or
something of the cantering measure of Adam Lindsay
Gordon, or even (curiously and not too often) a hint
of Matthew Arnold—but the general impression is
of an original force employing a method of his
own.

I think I have read all these narrative poems of
yours.   " The Everlasting Mercy " was the first.   It
is a tribute to the solid qualities of our race that, at
all events in some quarters, iis good qualities were
recognized.   Because you were never of those who
aim at making a good show at the start.   You do
not go in for " window-dressing."   It has generally
been your amiable practice to make the reader wade

through several pages of mere doggerel before you begin to scatter a pearl or two as reward. This, for instance, is typical of the first few pages of the story of Saul Kane.

> From '41 to '51
> I was my folk's contrary son ;
> I bit my father's hand right through
> And broke my mother's heart in two.
> I sometimes go without my dinner
> Now that I know the times I've gi'n her.

I have sometimes wondered whether this sort of exordium may not have a considerably higher value than appears on the surface. The writer's method, in short, is that of the purple patch. He just goes on, pouring out the most care-free verse imaginable, inventing a name when he has not got a rhyme to hand, not worrying in the least about an occasional plunge into muddy depths from which the customary poet would shy like a frightened horse, until at last he comes to something that fires his imagination. Then, suddenly, the reader gets an inspired passage, shining all the more brightly by contrast with what has gone before. When the fight comes on, and Saul looks round the ring and sees the " five and forty human faces " that have come to see him knocked out he feels a spite at them all :

> Faces of men who'd never been
> Merry or true or live or clean;
> Who'd never felt the boxer's trim
> Of brain divinely knit to limb,
> Nor felt the whole live body go
> One tingling health from top to toe.

There, on the fourth page, comes the first hint of a triumphant phrase.

L

It may be admitted that in " The Everlasting Mercy " there is a great deal of irrelevant stuff that we could very easily do without, and too many couplets of this sort :

> There's that Saul Kane, the drunken blaggard,
> Talking to little Jimmy Jaggard . . .

or

> His mother's gone inside to bargain,
> Run in and tell her, Polly Margin !

and not so many inspired lines as we should like to find.

Then came " The Widow in the Bye Street " and " Dauber." This story of the ship's painter who was also the ship's butt, the scorn of all because he had a sense of beauty and tried to set it down on canvas in his spare hours, until he found his manhood working aloft with the rest in a gale off the Horn, was the first that I remember seeing seriously criticized in the Press. There is more poetry in it than in any of the rest—the poetry of the sea, peaceful in the tropics and lashed to fury down by the Horn.

" The Daffodil Fields " is a tragedy, a bloody tragedy indeed. " Rosas " is hardly less stained with murder. But then we come to that excellent piece of cantering verse, " Reynard the Fox," which I beg leave to consider, up to the present, your *chef d'œuvre* in narrative verse.

This " Reynard the Fox " is a glorious piece, in its way. Amazingly full, like a turbulent stream in flood time, carrying with it all sorts of incongruous material gathered in its headlong rush. You seem to have put down in it all that you know of fox-hunting, all that you have seen and heard and guessed. I

know of no description anywhere in verse which makes
the reader see and feel the scene so clearly. And
the opening page, this time, strikes the right note.
That preliminary picture of the activity at " The
Cock and Pye, By Charles and Martha Enderby,"
before the meet, must appeal to every one who has
ever lived in a hunting country.

> A pad-groom gave a cloth a beating,
> Knocking the dust out with a stake.
> Two men cleaned stalls with fork and rake,
> And one went whistling to the pump,
> The handle whined, ker-lump, ker-lump,
> The water splashed into the pail,
> And, as he went, it left a trail,
> Lipped over on the yard's bricked paving . . .

Cannot we hear and see the whole action ? It may
not be a great thing to describe the filling of a bucket
at a pump, but it is something to do so in a way that
sets us all aglow with the sensation of being there in
the yard ourselves, waiting for the hounds. What
other hand would have made the pump-handle whine
so convincingly ? The whole description is wonderful—but I must admit that you seem quite unable to
leave anything out. There are whole pages of these
scattered notes of sights and sounds in the stable
yard, mingled with little patches of conversation among
grooms and ostlers. Then a whole series of vignettes,
hastily dashed down, of the various followers of the
hunt as they assemble. Done almost roughly, as
though you disdained taking the least trouble over
such a catalogue, yet with a flash now and then of
insight or a phrase that gleams like a jewel in the
dark. I have wondered sometimes how far this
appearance of roughness is deliberately assumed.

There are the abruptest turns and transitions here and there, the most startling parentheses :

> Next came the Colways' pony-cart
> From Coln St. Evelyn's with the party.
> Hugh Colway, jovial, bold and hearty,
> And Polly Colway's brother, John
> (Their horses had been both sent on),
> And Polly Colway drove them there.
> Poor pretty Polly Colway's hair !
> The grey mare killed her at the brook
> Down seven springs mead at Water Hook
> Just one month later, poor sweet woman.
> Her brother was a rat-faced Roman . . .

And so forth.   Did man ever see a series of irrelevances lugged in by the heels in such fashion before ? And yet, in some curious way, it has its value.   Certainly there has never been a picture like this done in verse before, so life-like a group collecting one by one, typical of the English country-side.   You can almost hear the horses' hooves squelching in the mud and smell the odour of dead leaves.

Huntsman and hounds come on.   Has the entry of the pack ever been bettered, or equalled, in verse or prose ?

> . . . Round the corner came the Hunt,
> Those feathery things, the hounds, in front
> Intent, wise, dipping, trotting, straying,
> Smiling at people, shoving, playing,
> Nosing to children's faces, waving
> Their feathery sterns, and all behaving,
> One eye to Dansey on Maroon.
>
>   .   .   .   .   .
>
> But Dansey on Maroon was death,
> So, though their noses roved, their feet
> Larked and trit-trotted to the meet.

I do not know whether to admire this most, or the

subtle change of stride, so to speak, with which you approach the Second Part. I have already quoted too much, but I must give this picture of the fox in the early morning, sleeping on his grassy shelf in the gorse before he is aroused.

> Deep in his dreams he heard the life
> Of the woodland seek for food or wife,
> The hop of a stoat, a buck that thumped,
> The squeal of a rat as a weasel jumped,
> The blackbird's chackering scattering crying,
> The rustling bents from the rabbits flying,
> Cows in a byre, and distant men,
> And Condicote church-clock striking ten.

I know no one else who could have written " Reynard the Fox." Whereas a good many might have got quite near " Right Royal." This was an attempt to do for the race-course (or rather the steeple-chase) what you had already done for the hunt. I cannot regard it as a success. It has its moments, but the bulk of it is very pedestrian stuff. The opening part is in sober decasyllabics—a metre that I cannot think suited to your genius. There is a patch of dialogue between the two lovers before the race which has always seemed to me quite unnecessarily tame :

> SHE. O grant they may, but think what's racing you,
> Think for a moment what his chances are
> Against Sir Lopez, Soyland, Kubbadar.
> HE. You said you thought Sir Lopez past his best.
> I do, myself.
> SHE. But there are all the rest.
> Peterkinooks, Red Ember, Counter-Vair,
> And then Grey Glory and the Irish mare.
> HE. She's scratched. The rest are giving me a stone.
> Unless the field hides something quite unknown
> I stand a chance. The going favours me.
> The ploughland will be bogland certainly .

and so forth. The fact is, there is too much of this
" sparring for time " about your verse ; you are apt
to put in anything that comes along in the hope that
soon something may strike a spark and set your
imagination ablaze. There are one or two good passages towards the end of " Right Royal," but it is
little better than a host of other descriptions of races
by far inferior artists.

I have spent all this space over your verse and
the prose will have to put up with a cursory valuation.
I do not care greatly for your " Gallipoli," which so
many critics praised so warmly. It seemed to me
you were less concerned there with what you had to
say than with the manner of your saying it—which
is unusual for you. I liked " Multitude and Solitude "
when I read it first, many years ago : " Sard Harker "
has a good deal about it that is very fine. I have
heard good judges say that some of the short things
in " A Mainsail Haul " are as good as anything you
ever wrote. And then, again, there are the plays.
Probably you will never be a popular playwright.
You have this unfortunate trend towards the tragic
that has ruined so many of our most promising writers.
We have " The Tragedy of Nan," which is a rustic
tragedy, and " The Tragedy of Pompey the Great,"
which is historic, and I am told they are both very
fine. Then there are also " Philip the King," which
I have read but not seen, and " Good Friday," which
I do not think has yet been produced ; neither of
these can be called exactly cheerful. Still, I imagine
that on the whole you have not done badly out of
your various activities.
You have, at any rate, the satisfaction of knowing

that you are one of the few who " really count," as
we say, in the republic of letters.   And although your
prosody is not impeccable, by our old ſtandards, you
have written a few sonnets that may live—if indeed
sonnets continue to be read at all.

Mr. Horace Annesley Vachell

Mr. Horace Annesley Vachell

I HAVE been following your career so long, my dear Vachell, that I begin to feel an almost proprietary interest in you and your often excellent work. Strange, this feeling ! I seem to have known you ever since those far-off days when you came back to your native country after ranching in California, and dived headlong into the waters of fame with " Brothers." It was a fine splash you made then, and deservedly : to my mind that book remains in some ways the best novel you have ever written. There followed " The Hill," and " Her Son," and " The Waters of Jordan," and many another. As the journalist says, you have never looked back since. In fact, you have pressed steadily forward, adding a theatrical paddock to the pleasant literary demesne you had conquered and occupied. There is a fund of perseverance in you that is bad to beat : if you make up your mind to succeed in any known branch of human activity I have no intention of laying any odds against you : the probability is that you will arrive there smiling in evening clothes, prepared to make an excellent reply to the toast of your health which the chairman of the congratulatory dinner is about to propose. Admirable Crichton as you are, after-dinner speaking comes also within your prehensile grasp.

I take it you can do most things that the Englishman of your age and station does—probably better
than most.   I picture you as pretty useful with a gun,
a good rider to hounds, somewhere near scratch as
a golfer, and still taking a friendly interest in more
strenuous ball games.   And I would make bold to
wager a respectable sum that your appointments
would be of the best in everything you took up.   The
second best would never be good enough for you if
by any means the best could be procured.   You
like to " do yourself well " all round.   And why
not ?   Most of us think with you on that point in
our hearts, but for some reason or another we keep
it dark.   Either we are forced to be economical, or
we wish to pose as anchorites.

Sanity is the outstanding characteristic of your per-
formance in literature.   I know no one who has
contrived to preserve so high a general level of sanity,
and yet escape dullness.   This, when you consider it,
is a great compliment ;   and without doubt it is the
secret of your popularity.   A large class of readers
exist who can appreciate humour, a touch of pathos
here and there (not too much of this), a well-constructed
and well-told story, and pleasant people.   They like,
in short, to be introduced into a nice social circle,
something like their own (or possibly a shade higher),
and to feel confident that nothing terrible is likely
to happen.   You are not one of these revolutionary
writers who aim at making every one so uncomfortable that the reader either throws his book violently
into the corner of the room or takes to serious thinking.   Yet you are not merely flippant and amusing.
These stories of yours are drawing-room comedies
with a purpose.   They are designed to infect the most

conservative of country gentlemen with the bacillus
of thought. He reads on, unsuspecting, deceived
by the air of good comradeship, the manifest appreciation of the good things of life, the little touches that
show the sportsman, the connoisseur of wine, the
Old Harrovian. " This fellow," he says, " knows
what he's about. Not one of those infernal Socialists.
I can trust him." And does trust him accordingly ;
so that when he chances to find remarks that might
be taken as bearing rather hardly on his own class he
is far more likely to pay heed to the warning than if
he had found the words in a story by John Galsworthy
or H. G. Wells.

There never was a more charming instructor of
the maiden aunt. I can see her now, purring gently
over " Blinds Down " or some similar work of yours,
her heart beating fearfully now and again as she
wonders whether you are not becoming—just a little
—risky. Of course she knows, like her brother the
Squire, that you are thoroughly to be trusted ; but
still, you see, there is that baby to be explained, and
the clergyman seems hardly the sort of man we should
like in our parish, and she certainly never heard
young Guardsmen talk quite like that when she was
a girl. Still, Mr. Vachell is eminently safe, and who
should know all these things if not he ? She reads
on and on, and the little touch of sentiment at the
end brings a happy mist before her pale blue eyes, and
she puts the book away in a corner of the case meaning
to lend it to dear Fanny when she comes back from
Harrogate. When a new book is announced by the
talented author of " The Other Side " you may be
sure her eyes will discover it in the columns of the
Morning Post before anyone else, and it is down on

her library list that same day.   I suspect you have
the suffrages of many a quiet country household, many
a discreet old-fashioned home under the shadow of
some famous cathedral, and probably every rector's
wife in the kingdom.   It is an enviable fate.

It is the more enviable because you do them good
all the time.   You educate them by stealth.   Unsus-
pectingly they suck wisdom from your works.   The
fact is, you stand precisely at the convenient level for
them.   You are not, and never were, one of these
pestilent enthusiasts who cannot preach without getting
violent and making every one so uncomfortable.   You
are broad-minded, but not too much so : you stand
perhaps twenty or thirty feet higher up the slope,
and your voice carries quite well over the intervening
distance.   It might be worth while climbing up that
far, whereas it would clearly be ridiculous to attempt
reaching the summit of that peak, whereon we can
dimly descry a ridiculous figure making unintelligible
signs.   You tell us the view is really better from
where you stand, and we can believe you : that fellow
is probably too high to see anything at all.

It is clear that you are the Heaven-sent interpreter
of modern views to that vast mass of inert obstruction,
the Tory of the old school.   In the New Forest,
where I am informed you reside, there must be plenty
of material for you : the flock are there, dyed deep
in the wool ; ready to listen to the shepherd, however,
if he also can claim to be a Forester.   That half forgotten corner of Hants is a fine preserve of the Old
School : in it you have discreetly laid the scene of
most of your works, peopling it with Mottisfonts and
Jallands and Pundles, not to mention that charming
family, the Verneys of Verney Boscobel, or that estim-

able baronet, Sir Geoffrey Pomfret of Nether Applewhite. I have wondered sometimes whether the Forest
manifests any apprehension at the announcement of
another novel from your prolific typewriter. No ! I
fancy not. You can be trusted to satirize none but
the right people—those who ask for it with no uncertain voice. And they are also (by a beneficent provision
of Nature) exactly those who would never recognize
their own portraits limned with a touch of caricature.

I can always read your novels with pleasure, though
I am quite prepared to admit that occasionally the
marks of your carpentry show a little too clearly. It
is an excellent thing to be an expert at contrivance,
so long as we do not suffer our mechanical ingenuity
to override everything else. I do not know, for this
reason, that play-writing is the best thing in the world
for your genius. About most of your later novels
there hangs the faint aroma of the stage : they read
sometimes as though they had been constructed with
an eye to the theatre ; and it is a fact that often before
they have appeared in print your busy machine is
already clicking them out in another form. Indeed,
it has been sometimes a matter of dispute among the
cognoscenti whether the book preceded the play, or
vice versa. The point is of no more than academic
interest.

As to the plays themselves, some few have been
successful, though it cannot yet be said that you are
as popular a playwright as you are a novelist. Your
judgment of what the public wants is, in short, less
infallible on the boards than between them. Yet it
would be a little difficult to say why. Your dialogue
is in general very good indeed. I am inclined to
think that your imagination is too fervid for the sober

dramatiſt. You piĉture in your own mind an ideal caſt, ſteering taĉtfully round the rather doubtful points, and never thoughtlessly over-ſtepping that razor-edge that separates the sublime from the ridiculous. If, as sometimes happens, you see them doing these things at rehearsal, I take it you assume that a few well-chosen words of remonſtrance will be sufficient to prevent such a contretemps occurring again. You were ever of a sanguine temperament.

"Quinney's," I suppose, is your beſt play, so far, as it is also one of your beſt books. And in it you were better served than usual by your caſt. But I confess I think the critics are generally far too severe about your dramatic work. They said a lot of hard things about your laſt—"Blinkers" it was called—queſtioning among other things the words you had put into the mouth of your old Colonel. Now I am prepared to bet a considerable sum that you were perfeĉtly right on that particular point, and that the dramatic critics were quite wrong. I would back your knowledge of the mentality of a retired colonel, living in Nether Applewhite or its neighbourhood, againſt that of any dramatic critic who ever lived.

"Blinkers" was a failure. I am sorry to see that you should have a failure, but perhaps these things are sent for a purpose, as my aunt used to say. An occasional set-back is probably good for you, spurring you on to greater efforts in the future. For you dislike being beaten. There is a glorious air, as of a Conqueror by Divine Right, about your daily dealings with the world. I expeĉt to see you emerge successful in the end from your ſtruggles with the hydra of the ſtage. Have you not fought with publishers in Albemarle Street and with editors all over the world, finally bending them to your will ? You are bound to win in the end—if only for the excellent reason that you tackle each new piece of work as though it were the one thing in the world that really wanted doing. I don't believe you have ever done a play, a story, or a sketch, without honestly believing at the time that it was the best piece of work you had ever turned out. And though subsequent reflection and the strictures of well-meaning friends may half convince you afterwards that you were mistaken, that does not prevent you from holding precisely the same belief over the next task you take in hand—and the next.

How excellent a thing it is to have a cheerful spirit, and a good digestion ! These are by no means your only good qualities, but I rate them as among your most valuable possessions. Two of your more recent books show you, it seems to me, at your happiest— your autobiographical memoirs, which you pleasantly call " Fellow-Travellers," and that delightfully contrived story of Brittany and middle-aged flirtation— " Change Partners." No one could have written those books who was not of a sunny disposition, who had not enjoyed life all through and done his best to make others enjoy it equally. And we can do with a little cheerful sanity in our novels to-day.

M

Mr. Charles Marriott

Mr. Charles Marriott

PERHAPS we may congratulate ourselves—we who take a serious interest in English literature—that the name of Charles Marriott remains, after many years of steady artistic endeavour, practically unknown to the crowd. Here and there, I suppose, one may stumble upon a little circle of your admirers, for even the least popular of us have generally our circle somewhere—if we could only find it. I discovered one of yours some years ago in a small and out-of-the-way seaside resort on the South Coast. The elderly lady who ran the local library, letting out novels at twopence a time, if I remember right, had a complete set of your works, as they existed at that date. I was the more struck by the sight of that row of volumes because the bulk of her shelves were given over to fiction of the most ordinary class.

I never succeeded in discovering why she had selected you for this mark of esteem. Curious as I am by nature in these matters, I was only able to elicit from her the fact that she liked reading you. But she confessed that you could not be called a popular writer. She had done her best, but the inhabitants and visitors at Bogness did not take to you as readily as she could have wished. " A bit too good, perhaps," was her discerning judgment. Possibly I raised myself some way in her esteem by taking out the whole list of your novels, in quick succession, thereby laying the foundation for that accurate knowledge of your earlier work that I shall disguise so successfully in these pages. From internal evidence I place that visit of mine to the seaside somewhere about 1908. I think "The Kiss of Helen" was the latest of yours that my friend the librarian had in stock.

But how fortunate, in a way, this fact that you have hitherto evaded popularity ! You skirted it, I suppose. "The Column" was your first book—or at all events the first of which I have cognizance—and "The Column," I imagine, sold better than anything you have written since. Some men would have " arrived " on the strength of that book, and gone on, encouraged by their agents and publishers, reproducing themselves ever since. By some good fortune you escaped, with nothing worse than a slight scratch. Perhaps it did not really sell much more than three or four thousand, after all. But a first novel that does as well as that has often been fatal.

In any case, there has been no real danger since. You have gone on steadily, writing your novels pretty regularly when you could spare the time from your other avocations. For you are also one of that strange band, the Art Critics, whose function it is to go round the innumerable galleries where painters, young or old, show their works. Yours it is, with the rest of your tribe, to " knock off " one or two of these picture-dealing propositions every few days, devoting to each its quota of praise or blame. I imagine you are apt to err on the side of generosity. There is not much acid in your disposition.

I sometimes wonder what would have happened had you been able to devote yourself to novel-writing with a single mind.   When I firſt knew you, some-where about the beginning of the century, you were turning out your ſtories annually with the precision and finish of a well-oiled machine.   Then there came a period of greater aċtivity, when you got into the way of producing two, or even three, in a single year. Consequently, though press of work in other direc-tions has checked your output during the laſt few years, you have already quite a respeċtable liſt of titles to your credit.   There is enough for a solid reputation. And yet, now and again even some of those who should know better look puzzled when your name is men-tioned among present-day Maſters of Fiċtion.   " Oh, yes, the Art Critic," they will say, or " Ah, you mean the man who writes about Architeċture, I suppose." Perhaps, if you had really been able to praċtise con-tinually on a single inſtrument you might by now be recognized as the legitimate successor to the late Henry James.

Your books, like his, have to be read carefully— which is probably why few even among the professional critics have ever done you juſtice.   Often, too, you deliberately take up a difficult ſtance, as when (in " The Dewpond " I think it is) you eleċt to write in the per-son of an unmarried woman.   It was something of a *tour de force* to keep that up all through the book, with-out ever losing the feminine touch proper to the sup-posed narrator.   I think you are generally good on women : the two uncommon types in that book were excellently done, well contraſted and well observed. They are drawn, like all your charaċters, obliquely, with a glancing treatment ; and I suppose the general reader does not care for this subtle method. What a number of your delicate hints of characterization and shadowy pearls of expression must remain unnoticed, buried in your pages, appreciated only by the rare collector. Yours are books for the novelist ; they make their appeal to brother craftsmen.

It is true enough that your novels will not live as stories. They are often just the slightest framework for the exhibition of a few characters, and for the introduction of sane and sensitive talk on such subjects as interest you—painting and architecture and music. I recollect, for instance, reading " An Order to View " not very long ago—a book which represents you at perhaps your slightest, and is therefore all the better as a specimen for examination : there is not too much tissue to dissect away before we get down to the structure. Here the setting was in Barstow and Cleeve, apparently meant for Bristol and Clifton. The hero is one Wedmore, a rising young architect who has just won the prize in a competition design for a Technical Institute, about to be given to the city by one Sir John Pumphrey, a rich profiteer. Wedmore gets engaged to Sir John's stately and brilliant daughter but going to view a little old manor house in the neighbourhood finds there a young woman who is obviously destined to be his mate. Fortunately Hilda Pumphrey is simultaneously attracted by her brother, a promising young musician, so that all ends as well as could be expected. But, as a plot for a novel, you will agree that there seems to be a certain lack of complication.

These books of yours, in short, are not so much novels as neatly constructed cabinets for the display of your collection of curiosities of character. When

I think of you at work I picture to myself a keen and
spectacled entomologist, roaming the fields with his
net, alert to capture a few more specimens of these
singular and fluttering animals that contrive to be so
extremely busy about so very little.   You do not take
much interest in the Ordinary Person : the characters
you prefer to draw must be strange, complex, elusive.
Take, for example, " The Grave Impertinence," which
I still preserve on my overcrowded shelves and look
through occasionally when I think I require a mental
tonic.   When I reviewed that book I remember
picturing your mild triumph as you got your net
fairly over Hugh Sadler, or George Penkevil, or General
Dunster, and managed to transfer the capture safely
and all but undamaged to the bottle.   For they are
all what we call cranks, these worthy gentlemen :
there is a screw loose in each of them somewhere—
not badly loose, but just enough to make them interesting studies to the naturalist.   And how cleverly
you exhibit them, though possibly your glancing
method is too elusive for the plain man.   Even the
title you chose was elusive.   You will not pretend
that the ordinary reader knows the works of Abraham
Cowley well enough to recollect that he wrote of
" Business, the Grave Impertinence " ; yet you no
doubt thought it a happy title for a business novel.
Perhaps you are now become a trifle stiff-necked in
your attitude towards popularity.   It is all very well
to write to please yourself, but one may make a few
harmless concessions.

I have rarely seen you " button up " a story in the
customary and presumably popular way.   Not many
of these novels end with the sound of wedding bells.
Some, like " Genevra," steer towards the cape of matri-

mony from the start, but, after a prodigious amount of tacking, contrive to sheer off at the finish again towards the open sea. The fact is, you are disdainful of the ordinary sentimental story : you are far more interested in these curious characters that you invent or discover. You delight in some obscure point of conscience : you place the intellectual value of your novels above the emotional. Which explains in part why you have never attained those pleasant slopes in the sun where graze the glorious company of the Best Sellers. Your books are for those who prefer to use their brains.

NO. XIX

Mr. William John Locke

Mr. William John Locke

IN the dark ages, when for my sins I was condemned to sojourn in the barbaric North—it was about the time that the once-famous Kailyard School were beginning to make something of a stir in the literary world—I used occasionally to hear the name I have set at the top of this paper as that of a clever young fellow, a master at Glenalmond, who intended to take up writing as a profession. I need not say how this interested me. I too was a master in a Scottish school : I also meant to write, was even then beginning in a tentative sort of manner, sending round quite unsaleable stuff to various editors and publishers. But this Glenalmond fellow was reported to be writing a novel, and I had not got to that length yet. A novel seemed to me a great undertaking, a setting forth on an adventurous voyage over a wild and uncharted sea. One might be lost there, never coming again to shore. Easy to begin a story, but in those days I could never see my way more than a chapter or two ahead.

I forget now which of my many colleagues was a friend of yours, but you must have impressed him with a sense of your superior ability. Anyway, I remembered your name. And soon after I left to come up to London and attack editors and publishers from closer quarters that first novel of yours appeared.

Somehow it happened that I got your next for review
—at least I think it was your next—" The Demagogue
and Lady Phayre " it was called.   I am pleased to
think that I spoke quite warmly of its considerable
promise.   I was new to the game then : besides, I
have always been of a kindly disposition.   Also, I
could not help feeling that I had a sort of proprietary interest in you.   You were the only novelist in
those far-off days, or nearly the only novelist, with
whom I could claim an acquaintance even at second-
hand.

Since then I have watched your steady ascent of
the ladder of fame with interest and occasional applause.
Your books not infrequently come before me for
judgment, and I am always glad when they do.   The
reader can have some confidence in a Locke.   He will
not, he may be pretty sure, be badly let down, though
I admit that I have one of your books on my shelves
that I have never been able to get through.   (I hasten
to add that it is one of your earlier works.)   I reviewed
" Derelicts " for some literary paper, now no doubt
deceased, and " The White Dove " (which is not one
of your best), and " The Morals of Marcus Ordeyne,"
which definitely placed you somewhere up on the
higher planes.   Strange, how there is always one
particular book, which may be neither better nor
worse than its predecessors, but brings to the fortunate writer fame and money, or at least a competence.
The critics, who have been waiting so long, measuring
and comparing, suddenly close their stop-watches with
a snap, note down the time and go to write their articles
on the arrival of a new star in the literary firmament.
" The Morals of Marcus Ordeyne "—it was dramatized afterwards and its name mercifully shortened

—was the book on which you " arrived." In those days the word was just coming into fashion.

It is not a little curious that Marcus Ordeyne should also have been a mathematical master at a school, and that he should have expressed in no uncertain manner a wholesome distaste for the job. I do not suppose that you could really have much enjoyed your period of probation up among the hills of Perth. The kindly gods sent you a pleasanter job as Secretary to the Royal Institute of British Architects, which you held for a matter of ten years. What an excellent post to fall into the lap of a young novelist who was just beginning to feel his way !

In 1906 came " The Beloved Vagabond."

The few critics who had not already signalled your " arrival " made haste to repair their omission. Sir Marcus Ordeyne (for this remarkable schoolmaster of yours succeeded to a baronetcy—perhaps the first of his profession to rise to so giddy a social height in fiction) began the good work of making you a popular favourite : Paragot continued it ; and, to tell the truth, a whole host of amiable but irresponsible vagabonds have been doing their utmost to make you a Best Seller ever since. I am not in the secrets of your publisher, but I suppose by now your books must be having a good enough sale. Without being a Hutchinson or an Ethel M. Dell, a novelist can sometimes manage to keep up an establishment on the Riviera.

This Beloved Vagabond idea has been worked very hard since it gave a title to that book. Indeed, if I remember right, there was an adumbration of him even in " Marcus." And since then, as I have heard some envious detractors hint, you have been almost unable to produce a novel without including a specimen

of this favourite type.   I don't suppose you do it from
malice prepense.   I mean to say, I have too high an
opinion of you to suppose that you are one of those
authors who deliberately choose the easy path to
success ; who, because they have hit the popular
fancy with one sort of book, allow themselves to be
persuaded by publisher or agent to repeat themselves
until they disguft their moft ardent supporters.   I
think you have a real humanity, a real sympathy with
joyous rogues, a real love for the quixotic crank.   But
when I think of the laft ten novels of yours that I
have read I confess I find in them a certain sameness.
I think you would be wise to break away from tradition
before it is too late.   For surely your popularity is
sufficient to carry the greater part of your admirers
anywhere you may elect to lead them.

   This popularity of yours is really rather remarkable,
and I have often been tempted to wonder how you obtained it.   When I meet (as I so often do meet) friends
from the country who take an intereft in literary affairs,
it is almoft always of you that they ask, and I can
tell by the intonation of their voice when your name
is mentioned what sort of a reverence you have inspired
in them.   " So you really know Locke ? " they say.
" W. J. Locke ?   Ah ! "   And the sigh that follows
tells me that somehow or other you have got down to
the great heart of the public as few of our generation
have.   It is gratifying, if a little aftonishing, to discover how real is the affeâion you inspire in some of
these ruftic breafts.   There muft be a reason for it—
a reason that a respeâable critic should be able to
trace to its source.   I mean, of course, apart from
your facile invention of charaâers like Septimus and
Ephraim Quixtus, Paragot and Ariftide Pujol.   And

if there is a reason there are many who will want to
know it. All my co-workers, for a certainty. Nobody
who has the least connection with the art and practice
of writing can afford to neglect a hint that may be so
valuable.

I fancy I can tell the humble seeker after popularity
what have been the chief reasons, the main secrets
of your success. That does not, of course, ensure
that he will be able to follow in the same path and
attain the same results. Success depends in the main
upon the possession of certain qualities which cannot
easily be acquired. The chief of these is sincerity. I
have always maintained that in order to become really
popular a novelist must believe thoroughly in his own
work. It is never the smallest use for him to write
with his tongue in his cheek—unless, of course he is
writing satire. Now you are sincere, just as the late
Marie Corelli was sincere. She may have made some
absurd mistakes, she may have laid on the colour so
lavishly that critics thought the effect ridiculous, but
there is no doubt she really intended to lash vice and
exalt virtue to the best of her ability.

In " The Coming of Amos " I notice that you
deliver yourself gravely of the apophthegm—" Insin-
cerity in Art is the Living Death." Miss Corelli
would have liked to set that down herself, but how few
of us others would have the courage to do so—seriously!
We should be afraid of being laughed out of our
club.

But, besides this matter of sincerity, which is perhaps
the chief thing, you possess two qualities that are not
found too often in combination. When they are, it is
almost safe to prophesy a certain degree of popular
success. You have a sufficient knowledge of the world,

N

combined with a real desire for what the Americans tersely and expressively call " uplift."   Knowledge of the world—especially of the gay world—is good, but not essential to popularity.   It can be simulated, and frequently has been : writers may really imagine they possess it, and their readers may not be sufficiently instructed to discover how remarkably shallow their knowledge is.   I have known popular writers whose aristocratic figures were frankly ridiculous : their dukes and marquesses were just capable of deceiving a servant girl : their lower ranks of the peerage were only a shade less impossible.   But as their reading public was almost entirely composed of servant girls this defect did not really matter : they continued blithely to present pictures of the *beau monde* that satisfied their remarkable circle, and sardonic critics sniggered in vain, unheard, except that the fortunate author, reading his morning bundle of press-cuttings, might exclaim on the ungenerous envy of small minds.   But you, I need hardly say, stand in a different category from those giants of my youth.

It is something, after all, to have been a schoolmaster, even in the wilds of Perth.   It means that you had a certain education ; and, in effect, turning up my old Cambridge University Calendar, I perceive that one Locke, of St. John's, went through the Mathematical Tripos of 1884, *non sine gloria*.   You displayed, that is to say, a certain power of adaptation that has enabled you, since, to put baronets, peers, and even Russian princesses into your books without altogether divorcing them from real life.   And this means that you are enabled to thrill the hearts of a class of readers a stage or two higher up the social scale than the admirers of the late Charles Garvice—

an excellent story-teller and one of the best of good
fellows, whose knowledge of earls, however, was
restricted to the (imaginary) fact that they wore belts.

And, finally, which is perhaps the most important
of all to a writer, you have the reputation of being, *au
fond*, on the right side. There are some who write
about the gay world who somehow contrive to leave
an unpleasant taste in the mouth, as though we too,
the humble readers, had been sitting up at the gaming
tables the night before, drinking liqueurs and smoking
more than was quite good for us. But with you we
are safe. Even those vagabonds of yours, who must
have been a little dubious at first sight to the mature
maiden lady, turn out at the end to be every bit as
lovable as we had heard. Yes, you are of that happy
band who can afford to skirt the borderland of wicked-
ness. A Cook's guide, as it were, to the *demi-monde*.
" Such a pleasant fellow, my dear, and so intellectual.
Something about his face that makes you feel how
superior he is to all that sort of thing. I should call
it almost a spiritual look. And so cheap, too—only
seven-and-six a trip ! "

Mr. Hugh Seymour Walpole

Mr. Hugh Seymour Walpole

STRANGE, is it not, to think that you are nearly twenty years my junior, and that already you have arrived at the dignity of a Collected Edition of Works, complete with portrait of the author on the wrapper and as frontispiece to each individual volume ! I am glad of the portrait, though it does not tell me very much. Like the late Thomas Carlyle, I like to study the lineaments of my hero of the moment. In the reproduction before me I perceive a decidedly lofty forehead, a pair of thoughtful eyes assisted in their task of continual observation by a pair of *pince-nez* glasses, a kindly, sensitive mouth that is no doubt capable of taking on a satirical smile. There is no moustache to conceal it when you decide to do so. On the whole, a pleasant face, as pictured by the well-known house of Elliott and Fry. I have seen another, by Mr. Hoppé, if I remember right, which resembles nothing so much as a dying fish. But then Mr. Hoppé is one of those photographers of genius who prefer to take it out of their sitters in this way.

I think you, or your publishers, made a sensible choice in sticking to the more commonplace presentation. Like the portrait of the great Robert Montgomery, which also was prefixed to one of his immortal

works, it appears to be doing its best to look like a
man of genius and sensibility, and with greater success
than the subject of Macaulay's vitriolic essay.   After
all, this is what the public expect of a popular author.
I confess freely that I shall probably try to look as
intellectual as possible myself when my publishers
tardily decide to ask me for a photograph.

How long is it now, I wonder, since the great Henry
James designated you as the imminent successor of
Thackeray ?   It must have been some time before
the war, I suppose, for I knew you then only as the
author of " Mr. Perrin and Mr. Traill," and I did not
quite see on what grounds the prophecy was based.
That rather gloomy study of the Schoolmaster with
Nerves had not struck me as indicating any immediate
apotheosis.   It was good enough, but nothing much
out of the common.   Still, I believed in Henry James
—up to a point.   I decided that I should certainly
have to keep a watchful eye on your future progress.
Two of your earlier works, " The Wooden Horse " and
" Maradick at Forty."   It might be worth while to
study these in order to detect, and isolate, the germ of
future greatness.

They tell me you wrote " The Wooden Horse "
while you were still at Cambridge, Emmanuel being
your college, but it was not published till 1909, when
you had attained the reasonable age of twenty-five.
It is certainly a most immature work.   If I had been
shown the book as the work of a young man, still an
undergraduate, I do not know that I should have been
inclined to anticipate too roseate a future for him.   It
would have impressed me, in a way.   I should have
thought the young man had been extraordinarily quick
at picking up the tricks of his trade, but had missed

laying hands on what really mattered. The opening
of the book, for example, might quite easily have been
written by the Walpole of to-day. But the characters
are, here and there, terribly wooden. Broadly speaking, you got the right types together. Old Sir Jeremy
Trojan, his son Harry, just back from New Zealand,
Garrett and Clare and the wanderer's son Robin—the
first view of this family party stimulates the interest
well enough. But as the story progresses their actions
and talk become less and less probable. Some of the
subsidiary characters are ridiculous throughout. But
I admit there are several redeeming features.

There are one or two passages that show the young
man had already some idea of writing. And your
sense of the ridiculous was not too acute. That is the
fatal thing, in youth—to be afraid of becoming ridiculous. You did not mind being a little absurd here
and there. You would use an old situation or an old
form of words without worrying too much about
them. They were conventions of the trade you had
decided to adopt—useful things to employ until you
had learned to get on without their assistance.

On the whole, wooden as it undoubtedly was,
" The Wooden Horse " was remarkable—for a first
novel by a Cambridge undergraduate. And in your
next I hasten to admit that you had improved out of
all knowledge. " Maradick at Forty " was a very
different affair indeed.

This book was published in 1910 and, though still
immature, showed a great deal of promise. A good
deal of it was derivative, and the careful student of
English fiction can trace it to its source if he cares to
take the trouble. But the central idea was a good one,
and the characters are infinitely better drawn than

those of the first book. Most of them are very nearly very good, but there is still a slight uncertainty about one or two. You had not yet quite got into your stride. Of all the characters I think Mrs. Maradick is the most successful—at all events the most consistent. But Tony is good, as the eternal spirit of Youth. Maradick himself has moments when we regretfully cease to believe in him. And Morelli— that scene in his house when he is told the secret of the wedding outrages all probability. It won't do, that scene : it breaks down and leaves us cold when it is meant to curdle the blood with horror. All the same, I am not saying that you were not perfectly right to attempt it. The young man who tries nothing that is beyond his powers will probably not go very far.

There is a touch of " Richard Feverel " about the courtship of Tony Gale and Janet Morelli (Maradick himself standing by in the rôle of the Old Dog). And in Garrick, commonly known as " Punch," there is a faint flavour as of one of Mr. Locke's pleasant vagabonds. As for Morelli, I have met with one or two attempts to put that amoral, faun-like gentleman into a book. I think Henry James must have helped you with him. He is very nearly a real creation.

As I have said, I did not think very much of the scholastic novel that followed. But it is interesting to note that you too have passed across that arid desert, teaching small boys in a Cornish school. I begin to think it may be useful, perhaps even necessary, as training for a future novelist. But it was " Fortitude," the next book but one, that really brought you to the front.

I have read " Fortitude " more than once, and I

consider it a very fine book to have come from a young man of less than thirty. It has a good central theme, and it shows signs of real power in places, and it is fairly well constructed. Peter Westcott is a good figure-head, consistently drawn, and Clare is excellent. But it is in the gallery of minor characters that I think the book chiefly succeeds. Most of them are good enough to remain in our memory for some time—and subsidiary characters in novels of the day do not generally live long with me. But I still remember Zanti, and Stephen Brant, and that quaint assistant in the bookshop (though I have forgotten his name for the moment), and old Mrs. Brockett who kept the boarding house in Bloomsbury, and Norah Monogue. I dare say I could remember more of them if I tried, as Cards and the Galleon family. A decidedly good book.

So far, you clung firmly to Cornwall. And then came the war, and tore you (as it tore most of us) from the safe anchorage that we had begun to imagine was ours for the rest of our time on earth. Out you went to Russia, to serve in the Red Cross, and as a result we have " The Dark Forest " and " The Secret City," and, no doubt, a very real development in the writer's own spirit. Anyhow, you were shaken out of a groove, which is no bad thing for us if it comes at the right time.

But I had nearly forgotten " The Duchess of Wrexe." Of the earlier books that is perhaps the best—better even than " Fortitude." It shows a greater mastery of material and of manner : there are moments when the reader is easily persuaded that he is sitting at the feet of a veritable creator, so assured is the style, so deft the construction. The Duchess herself, how effective is that opening introduction of her portrait in the gallery, with Felix Brun, the sharp, inquisitive, bird-like man for chorus, the explorer Arkwright, Lady Adela and Rachel Beaminster all fortuitously gathered together there to inspect the work ! I do not know whether you moved in those exalted circles yourself, but you certainly supplied a credible atmosphere : the plebeian reader felt that this Beaminster household had an air. Some dukes, and duchesses, must be like that—or must have been in the past. For this is a study of the close of the Victorian era. Practically it ends on Mafeking night. The very mention of Mafeking night now sets one almost wondering.

I think the characters in this book more human than any you had drawn up to that time. The ducal family were quite good, the three men pleasantly differentiated with a few deft strokes, Lady Adela a little stiff—but then she was meant to creak a little—Rachel and the old Duchess herself excellent. Then there are a number of secondary figures who are eminently likeable—Dr. Christopher, for example, and Lizzie Rand with her mother and sister, and Roddy Seddon—but he marries the leading lady so we can hardly class him as a secondary figure. Francis Breton is perhaps the least successful of all. But there again you were trying something difficult with Francis. He was credible for the greater part of the book : in the big confession scene in Roddy's room he seemed to fail. At any rate to my eyes he was not so credible as he had been.

I do not think the writing very good. You found your sense of character, I take it, before you formed your style. There is a certain lack of repose, a snappiness about your paragraphs. But this was the modern touch at that time. The new halfpenny Press (as it was then) had taught us that the modern reading public could not endure anything solid—anything even that looked solid. Sentences had to be short, for fear the attention of a bored student should wander and fail to return.

But you contrived to insert some passages of real beauty nevertheless. I liked your excursion into the society of the Autocrats, as Felix Brun described them. It was clear then that you were really worth watching. I intend to note your progress with all the scientific interest at my command.

What are you going to do next ? By what glorious star in the literary firmament are you going to set your course ? Lately it has been the *sidus Trollopium*, the Barsetshire constellation. Perhaps you had noted signs of a revival of interest in the bearded Anthony : perhaps you felt that in matters ecclesiastical the son of a bishop (once Examining Chaplain to His Grace the Archbishop of York) had opportunities that had been withheld from a mere official of the Post Office. At any rate you set to work some little time ago to build up a Polchester that should be the modern equivalent of Trollope's Barchester—a Barchester with all the most modern improvements. If you could not produce an accurate picture of a modern cathedral city, who could ?

" The Cathedral " had merit : " The Old Ladies " was not, to my mind, quite worthy of you. I do not feel that you cared much what became of the three poor old things that you had arranged beneath your microscope. They were just specimens that you had discovered in your new trawling ground. You were interested in the greedy specimen—a rather unusual capture this. You thought you saw a good touch, something that would send almost a thrill of terror through your less strong-minded readers, in the death of the poor weak specimen under the bullying domination of her companion. But it seemed to me that the book lacked sincerity.

You stand aloof, an observer, mildly interested in the figures you arrange on your little stage. You have a certain sense of the drama, and can construct your stories not unimpressively. But there is something a little cold and formal about your more recent work. The late Samuel Butler would perhaps have said that you had attained γνῶσις at the expense of ἀγάπη. (Since critics first began to write they have pointed out the enormous difficulty of handling this intractable pair so as to give each his due share of the work.) True that an artist must master his technique before he can express himself to the satisfaction of his hearers : equally true that in trying to gain this power the artist gradually loses the desire to say anything of real importance. There comes a time when your master of technique succumbs to the temptation of merely displaying the ability he has acquired.

Mr. Edward Frederic Benson

Mr. Edward Frederic Benson

THERE is something about the life of an English beneficed clergyman, I begin to think, that inclines his progeny towards a literary career. Perhaps it is merely that the children of the rectory imbibe insensibly a certain respect for letters. In the days of my youth we listened dutifully in church to the Psalms of David ; we heard the lessons read at least twice every Sunday ; we had the privilege of listening to innumerable sermons founded on the best models and often actually constructed from their material. And, during the week, we had generally a tolerable library on which to browse when there was nothing else of real importance to be done. Along with Horne's Introduction to the Scriptures, Prideaux's Connection, and the works of the judicious Hooker, we were tolerably sure to find a few half-forgotten volumes of early Victorian fiction or poetry. I recollect some bound volumes of an ancient magazine —I think it was the *Penny Magazine* or some such improbable name—in which I discovered more than one serial novel. " Frank Fairleigh " was among them. But enough of delving in the distant past.

Take it as we may, a fair proportion of my little gallery here are sons of clergymen—as, indeed, I am myself. And it is not without a certain pride that I regard their work. Two of them, actually, are sons of bishops : you yourself had for father an Archbishop of Canterbury, not the least famous of a famous line. Behind your banner (with that of Hugh Walpole fluttering close behind) we others may march contentedly at the tail of the long procession. J. D. Beresford will be somewhere there, and R. S. Hichens, and perhaps Sir Anthony Hope Hawkins—unless I find that I am making too much room for my own contemporaries. But much as I admire the younger generation, I do not see why we should let them have things all their own way.

This outburst of fiction in clerical circles must be something comparatively new. The great novelists of the past—Scott and Dickens and Thackeray, Wilkie Collins and Charles Reade and George Eliot—had no particular connection with the Church. (It is true that Mr. Evans was stated to have been " a churchman of the old school," which is something.) Stay, though ! there were the Brontës, and, in mid-Victorian days, the Kingsleys, and Tennyson—not that he was a novelist—and James Anthony Froude, who was the son of an archdeacon, and did write at least one novel. But I cannot remember a time when the ranks of our novelists were so closely packed with clerical offspring as they are to-day.

If I were asked to point out the best workman among our novelists now, I should probably give your name. This is not, I need hardly say, tantamount to classing you at the top of the innumerable practitioners who crowd our libraries. What I mean is simply that you have learned your trade pretty thoroughly since you first sprang into public notice with " Dodo," in 1893. And that book also showed that you had a certain aptitude for the game. You were quick to recognize that the son of an archbishop had opportunities that were denied to sons of a mere minor canon. A slight shock to the proprieties delivered from his pen came with a far greater impetus. " Dodo " was emphatically the right book for you to start with if you meant to make an early impression. You made it—and the remarkable thing is that you have managed to survive it. At the present moment you are probably the best constructor of tales we possess.

A writer requires more than mere skill in carpentry to produce a great novel. That is incontestably true, and I do not consider it in the least likely that you will ever write anything like one. But you have steadily gone on producing through a number of years a large number of very readable, well-written, well-constructed stories. I cannot recall reading anything of yours recently that has disappointed me— seriously. But there are some circles with which you deal better than others. I used to be a little uneasy sometimes in the past when you strayed momentarily from your customary pasture, writing books like " The Vintage " or " The Luck of the Vails." We preferred to regard you as the last and best authority on the London society of your day, whether it was the peeress in Mayfair or the commercial climber starting at Notting Hill and intending to finish in some magnificent mansion in Belgravia.

I suppose your career is a standing example to the young novelist of what can be accomplished by sheer practice. Given a young man with a certain power of observation, brains of a rather more than average swiftness of comprehension, and the slightly repressive atmosphere of an archbishop's household for your early upbringing, this is what you might be expected to arrive at if you kept steadily at your task. It is greatly to your credit that you have always worked carefully. Many men in your position would have been induced to turn out their fiction at top speed while the fame of " Dodo " was still the talk of suburban tea-tables and beginning to penetrate as far as the country rectory. But you have never overdone the thing : in the matter of " output," as agents and other commercialized hangers-on of literature term it, you were content for many years with little more than a single annual volume. And the happy consequence is that you have lasted these thirty odd years considerably better than some of your contemporaries.

What a number of your books I must have read since the papers were full of gossip about the heroine of that first book of yours, and rumours of " The Souls " reached me even in the wilds of Scotland ! I remember reading " The Rubicon," and, of course, " The Babe, B.A.," some of which had already appeared in the *Granta*, but after my time. I suppose we must have overlapped for a year at Cambridge, but I never knew many King's men, and I fear I was at least two years senior to you. (It is a sad fact that I find myself senior now to most of these writers whom I have made it my business to lecture.) Then I came to the conclusion that you were worth reading if there was nothing better to do, and I suppose I managed to beg or borrow most of your succeeding books until the time came when they were sent to me for review. I recollect reading " Vintage " and " Mammon and Co." (one of your best, I think), and " The Challoners." But I confess freely that I cannot remember

very much about any of these now. It is only by
referring to several cuttings from old papers that I
can even recall what I thought of those novels of yours
which I have reviewed.

Vaguely I recollect " The House of Defence,"
which dealt with Christian Science, and contained a
breezy American professor whom I rather liked.
Then there came three quite good specimens in a row
—" The Climber," " Daisy's Aunt," and " The
Osbornes." At least, I am not quite sure now about
the middle one of the three. I have a vague impression that it contained an aunt who flirted violently
with a young man in order to preserve a favourite
niece from marrying him. The scene was laid somewhere up the river, and the breakfast-table conversation was decidedly reminiscent of the " Dodo " era.
This gift for light badinage is one that you have
retained right down to the present day.

In " The Osbornes " it seems to me that you made
a gallant attempt to show that you really had some
sympathy with the wealthy manufacturer who has
risen from the ranks. There was an aristocratic
young lady who married into the Osborne family and
actually learned to love them the more through her
appreciation of their ridiculous points. This was an
interesting aspect of the case, and one that you had
not handled before : I perceive that it recalled to
me the saying of George Meredith : " You may
estimate your capacity for the comic by being able to
detect the ridicule of those you love, without loving
them less." There was something more sympathetic
than common about your handling of Mr. and Mrs.
Osborne.

Perhaps you will regard all this as somewhat faint

eulogium for a man of your undoubted eminence in
the profession of letters.   And yet it is really a good
deal to say.   Of how many novelists to-day can we
truthfully say as much?   I always take up a new
Benson with a feeling that I shall probably find something in it worth reading.   I know no living novelist,
grazing on the lower slopes (for I cannot put you
quite on a level with the three or four who have managed to get a footing somewhere near the peak), who
proceeds round his mountain (nibbling here and there
a succulent patch) at so equable a pace and so steadily
level a height.   And they are not too much like each
other, these novels of yours :   they are not by any
means all cut to the same pattern.   With each recur-
ring book, it seems to me, you take a surprisingly
fresh view of life.   I do not know that you are much
interested in the story.   Plots do not give you sleepless nights.   But you do get interested in your characters, and we can forgive much in any novelist who
does that.   They are generally quite life-like—for
the moment.   It is true that they seldom remain in
the mind for long after the book is finished.   Just
one or two may—a choice selection from your happiest
creations.   But somehow or other I have generally
found that your books do not linger in the memory.
They are eminently readable at the time, and we are
not ungrateful :   we like the characters well enough,
but we are not particularly anxious to meet them
again.

The fact is, you are better as a rule in the minor
characters than when you come to deal with your
protagonists.   Your thumb-nail sketches are better
than your big canvases.   In the last book of yours
that has come into my hands for review this is as true

as ever, though the novel itself is not at all in your usual line. This was " Alan," which professed to deal with one Alan Graham, described on the wrapper of the book as a " novelist of the old school." And indeed I have never met in my varied acquaintance quite so terrible a fellow as this. If the novelists of the old school are indeed in the least like Alan it will be a fine thing for the world when they die out. He seemed to me rather like a caricature of the chief character in Mr. Maxwell's novel, " The Guarded Flame," but even more thoroughly filled with unconscious egoism. And he spoke throughout the book as though he were dictating one of his own novels, dealing out his mellifluous and polished phrases as though the whole world were an Academy of Letters. I did not care much for Alan Graham, nor did I think his wife Agnes was entirely successful, nor the representative of the modern, post-war school of fiction, the young cousin Timothy, who has imbibed in the trenches a certain respect for violence and a rooted distaste for the sort of writing that is ferociously literary and nothing else. That is to say, they were all competently done, but I did not feel that in coming across them I had met strangers whom I should be likely to remember for any length of time. I was never startled or persuaded out of my critical faculty.

On the other hand, some of the minor figures were very good. I should like to meet Pamela Probyn again, busy with collecting lions and so delightfully ready to drop her old ones as soon as there is a chance of discovering and appropriating one whose claws are only just beginning to appear. And I liked Henry Blewitt, the literary critic, and Agnes Graham's Dodo-like sister.

I shall be sorry when you cease to entertain us—if I am still here. It is something to have a popular novelist who is also a respectable scholar, who is unlikely to make the grosser grammatical errors or to use words in their wrong meanings. And for the rest, are you not a champion figure-skater and one of the pillars of Winter Sport in Switzerland? I believe we are even fellow-members of the same distinguished golf club. But I need hardly say that this is not the sole reason for my including you in this even more distinguished gathering.

Mr. John Collings Squire

Mr. John Collings Squire

I PERCEIVE that you received your early education, or some share of it, at the famous old school of Blundell's, down Tiverton way, where also John Ridd had his firſt fight. The foundation of that eminent merchant, Peter Blundell, has several close scholarships at the two Universities—at Balliol, Oxford, and Sidney Sussex, Cambridge—but you did not apparently avail yourself of these. You went up to St. John's, Cambridge, as an hiſtorical scholar not long after the opening of the present century. And it was there, I suppose, that you began to exercise seriously the gift of parody that seems to come naturally to so many Cambridge men.

The man who can parody well is clearly the beſt critic. It is the critical faculty, conjoined with a sense of fun and a quick apprehension of the ridiculous, that makes your great parodiſt. Perhaps there is something in the soil or the air of Cambridge that ſtimulates the growth of this particular sort of mind. But I do not know whether you followed the common course of Cambridge poets, and wrote light verse in the *Granta*. Perhaps you developed later. I have no record of those early days.

Still a young man, scarcely more than forty, you have an enviable reputation as a Man of Letters.

Looking backwards, it seems to me to have sprung up with extraordinary rapidity, almost like a gourd in the night.   The name of Squire (with that of his faithful Shanks) stands now almost for a complete section of the literary world : it connotes just that group which decided, some ten years ago, to take their literature seriously ; and, if possible, to induce others to do the same.   The irreverent generally refer to this group as " high-brows," using a convenient Americanism : somehow or other it is popularly supposed that you are their high priest.   But it is a little difficult to discover by what stages you arrived at that position.

The *New Statesman* gave you, I imagine, your first real step in rank.   This paper stands for almost everything that is most repugnant to the opinions of the average, honest, brainless Englishman, but it has always maintained a more than respectable literary standard.   You became literary editor of it in 1913, and carried it on as acting editor during the two concluding years of the War.   Fresh from that you went to contest Cambridge University, in the Liberal interest, in the election of 1918.   I imagine you still have Parliamentary ambitions.   You became a Member of the Academic Committee in 1921, and Secretary the year after—a post for which you must be admirably fitted.   Academies were invented for men of your build and make.

When the late Sir William Robertson Nicoll passed away you stepped into his place without unnecessary loss of time as chief of the reviewing world.   I do not know that you employ quite so many aliases as that distinguished Aberdonian, but literary rumour insists that your opinion carries a good deal of weight.   Then again are you not the founder and editor of the *London*

Mercury ?   I do not pretend to know how the *Mercury* is doing now, but it started off from the porch at a good pace, the guard blowing a challenging fanfare on his yard of tin.   These magazines that profess to cater for the intellectual sections of society have their difficult period commonly after the first two or three years, when to the outside spectator they seem to be fairly settled in popular favour.   At first they are the fashion, the latest thing in the world of letters ; and all that nondescript population that hangs on the fringe of literature buys them to see what is going to be the next subject of conversation in really intellectual circles.   Frankly, I do not quite know what to think of your bantling now that it has grown out of long clothes.   I thought at first that we were going to get a real magazine—something that would strengthen the little band of old-timers that do still occasionally publish some story with a literary touch in it—but lately I have been rather disappointed.   Or perhaps it is merely that I am growing old.

I liked your own stories, which appeared from time to time in the *Mercury* and elsewhere about a year ago.   I can read anything you write with a certain pleasure.   It is, of course, an intellectual pleasure rather than an emotional.   You do not set out, I imagine, to touch the heart.   I like you best in your parodies, which are excellent, and in your Essays at Large (not quite so well in these) ; generally I think you are better in your derivative work than when you attempt to stand by yourself.   Yours is a creeper-like talent, demanding something like a trellis to support it if it is to flower freely.   This it is to be a critic by nature.   The trail of the critic lay clearly over " The Grub Street Nights Entertainments," which is the latest book of yours that I have seen. The short stories of which this collection consists are all stories of literary life. They keep closely to the world with which you are best acquainted, and are probably all the better for that fact. But it must be admitted that there is a certain similarity about your subjects and about the manner in which they are handled. I liked best the story of the poet in " The Cemetery " who was entrusted with all the obituary notices for a great daily paper, and won for himself a century or two of fame by means that the ordinary reader would never expect. There is something here that touches a weak spot in all of us who write. Perhaps you yourself may stumble on a partial immortality by some piece of work that seems to you as nothing : perhaps I may do the same by painfully writing this jejune sketch of your career. So great a gamble is the Life Literary—as the late Miss Marie Corelli liked to call it—and therein lies, I have always maintained, its chief charm.

You are, they tell me, occasionally to be found on the cricket field. It is an amiable weakness, with which I have considerable sympathy. But I am informed that in your case the pen is decidedly mightier than the bat.

Mr. Percy White

I DEBATED for some time, my dear White, whether I should select your name for my final lecture. You are not, I agree, very much in the public eye at the moment. Time was, I suppose, when you had a sort of fashion. You were the novelist of Park Lane and the West End (indeed had you not written two excellent novels to which those inspiring names had been attached ?). Suburbia, it was agreed, trembled at your nod : Surbiton had never been quite the same since you started your satirical career. But these triumphs, considerable as they were, belong to the past. It is some time now since your name was really familiar to the librarians in Kensington and Mayfair. We are, unfortunately, growing old.

At the same time, I do not see why we should tamely accept the verdict of our young critics, and acknowledge ourselves altogether inferior to the writers who have sprung up since the dividing line of the Great War. Very possibly they regard us as effete, back numbers, men with no message for the present generation. That may be ; but their judgment is not infallible. Besides, I am estimating you, not so much on the basis of your work during the last ten years as on that of the days when we were both young and full of pleasant enthusiasms.

How old are you now ? Upon my word, I cannot hazard a guess within ten years. All I know is that when I first met you, just about thirty years ago, I took you for a retired cavalry officer. You did not look much older when I came across you last year. But it is true enough that you have been a novelist since 1893, and that you began your journalistic career as long ago as 1880. To young writers who first saw the light somewhere near the beginning of the twentieth century these dates seem, of course, prehistoric ; they can hardly bring themselves to believe that it is worth while discussing the works of a gentleman who began writing in the early eighties. I can only repeat, with apologies, that you bear as yet few signs of senile decay. I read a little time ago " Mr. Bailey-Martin, O.B.E.," which was published first in March, 1923, just thirty years after the " Mr. Bailey-Martin " that made you famous and Surbiton furious, and it seemed to my partial mind that it was very nearly if not quite as good as its predecessor. You have still the old urbanely satirical manner, and can make pretty practice at flying folly with your barbed arrows. But there is only the slightest dash of poison on your shafts. You have always been a kindly satirist at heart, impaling your victims tenderly, as though you loved them.

A good many novelists have been schoolmasters : few have reached the dignity of Professor, but you are among the select band. Many years ago you were Professor of English Language and Literature at a certain French college, where you acquired that mastery of the Parisian accent that has been so long the envy of your numerous friends. That was even before you took up journalism, in 1880, writing leaders

for provincial papers (as George Meredith had done
before you), and editing *Public Opinion* for a matter
of ten years.   And now once again you have assumed
the gown, as Professor of English Literature at the
University of Cairo.   An unpleasant place in which
to dwell, in these times of unreſt !   But your
admirers may take heart : the vacations are mercifully long.

This professorial occupation has its uses.   I like
my writers to have a scholarly touch.   And you have
never been one of those authors who annoy the under-
paid critic with slovenly grammar or careless syntax.
Yours is a pleasant, easy and cultured ſtyle.   And you
have a good sense of charaćter : we do not often find
wooden puppets in your ſtories.   Your novels are
concerned with ordinary people, drawn commonly
from the upper middle class, and differentiated from
their fellows chiefly by the possession of a certain
talent for repartee.   Your conſtrućtion is good, your
dialogue brisk and lively, and you are usually well
up to date : if there is a " topic of the moment "
it is quite probable that some discussion on it
will be found in your lateſt novel.   A dispassionate
discussion, for you do not take sides : you merely
observe and record.   Perhaps you would have
enjoyed a larger sale if you had been more of a
partisan : perhaps also you would have made fewer
friends.

For you have never been among the big sellers of
your day.   Yours is a fair circulation, but no more :
your reputation has generally been in advance of your
sale.   The circle to which your books appealed was
something above the average in intelligence, but with
no great purchasing power.   A good library public,

but no more.   Yet you made an encouraging start in
fiction.   Your first novel, the " Mr. Bailey-Martin "
of which I have already spoken, was not only a success
with the critics ; it sold, I should say, a great deal
better than any book you have written since.   To
begin with your biggest success is always rather a
disappointing business for an ambitious author, but
it is no doubt better than never to enjoy a success at
all.

For a first novel, " Mr. Bailey-Martin " was
remarkably mature in style.   There is nothing of the
brilliant amateur about it ;   clearly its author was
born to write—teethed, let us say, on a gilt pen.   His
eponymous hero was a suburban snob, endowed with
the climbing instinct, determined to get on in the world,
and prepared to sacrifice a great deal (including his
first love) in order to do so.   Decidedly not a lovable
character, but by no means inhuman.   It could be
seen that the novelist had even a certain sympathy
with his creation : he would not then suffer him to
be altogether overwhelmed with disaster.   (When
he revived him as an elderly Silenus after the war
it was a different matter.)   Percival Bailey-Martin
had outlived such early charm as he may once have
possessed.

You have generally maintained this dispassionate
attitude towards your characters.   You do not lay
undue stress upon the less amiable qualities, nor do
you wax enthusiastic over the personal charms of your
creatures.   In fact, you have always written like a
kindly man of the world, taught by experience that
heroes are seldom entirely heroic or villains thoroughly
vile.   You like to pose as the elderly friend of the
family, perhaps with a sentimental attachment to the

wife, as in " Park Lane." I regard this as one of
the best of your books. Its atmosphere is admirable.
I should like to suggest that in future ages it should be
preserved as a faithful picture of a certain section of
London society about the time of the South African
War.

I think you mellowed as you grew older : there
came to you more humanity, more of the milk of human
kindness. To some happy mortals advancing age
brings this, and it is a liberal compensation for many
disabilities. For in the end it is the personality of
the writer that counts, and we love the kindly satirist.
Let him have, if you will, a touch of the corrective
acid of cynicism. The bitterness of the soured man
alienates all but the few who are of like mind with
him. You have never been soured, though perhaps
you have never quite reached that position which
your first book promised. Still, you have not done
badly—better than a great many of us—and you are
a philosopher. Perhaps you owe that also to your
professorial experience.

I propose to conclude here my little series of lectures.
There are many others whom I should have liked to
include—several who certainly ought to have been
included could I have found the time or my publisher
the space. Perhaps I may deal with some of them
on a future occasion. For instance, I have not
addressed a single lady—and every one who knows
anything about the literary world is aware that our
women writers rule the kingdom of fiction almost
unchallenged. Originally, I admit, there was in my
collection a lecture to a famous female novelist, but it
seemed almost an insult to include only one solitary

specimen among this herd of men. It is clear to me that the ladies are worthy of a volume all to themselves, if they are worthy of mention at all. What would one lecture be among so many?

And then, again, I have not included (no doubt I shall be told) any of the younger men, the bright hopes of English literature. Where are the Sitwells, Aldous Huxley, Michael Arlen and the rest? Well —I propose to wait and see where they will be in another five or ten years. No! if I had included any more they would have been drawn from the same old school—men who had done some real work, who had sown their wild oats and settled down, who could show something on which one might pronounce judgment. What is the good of composing a considered opinion on your Infant Phenomenon? (Let me add, for I am nothing if not frank, that I am not profoundly versed in these modern writers of ours.) I have always imagined myself to possess a catholic taste, but I confess that some recent successes have left me mildly astonished. Sometimes I feel that these new young men are talking a different language altogether from mine. I do not know what they are trying to do, at what far-off goal they may be aiming. Now with my good old friends of the past there need be no such doubts. A man should be careful about judging any but his own epoch.

But what a host there are who might have been added to my list! Surely there must have been a vast number of capable writers born during the last forty years of the nineteenth century. (The sixties, I cannot but think, were an exceptionally good period.) But I am not going to attempt a catalogue of names. Let it suffice that I have selected here those authors whose work I know best.   I have said what I thought of all—I trust without offence.   And if by any chance any of them think I have been unkind, let them turn to the illustrations, and be comforted !